The Adoption Option

THE
ADOPTION
OPTION

ANGELA ELWELL HUNT

VICTOR BOOKS®

A DIVISION OF SCRIPTURE PRESS PUBLICATIONS INC.
USA CANADA ENGLAND

Most Scripture quotations are taken from the *Authorized (King James) Version* (KJV). Other quotations marked (NIV) are taken from the *Holy Bible, New International Version.* Copyright 1973, 1978, 1984, International Bible Society. Used by permission of Zondervan Bible Publishers.

Recommended Dewey Decimal Classification: 362.734
Suggested Subject Heading: ADOPTION

Library of Congress Catalog Number: 88-62866
ISBN: 0-89693-667-8

© 1989 by SP Publications, Inc. All rights reserved. Printed in the United States of America. No part of this book may be used or reproduced in any manner whatsoever without written permission except in the case of brief quotations in critical articles and reviews. For information write Victor Books, P.O. Box 1825, Wheaton, IL 60187.

Contents

To Joe and Ann Hale,
Dennis and Susan Lugar
with
overwhelming gratitude
and love

Foreword

The resurgence of the pro-life movement has begun to emphasize an area about which Christians have been too silent—adoption. In *The Adoption Option*, Angie Hunt has portrayed adoption as a miraculous, loving way of adding to a family.

As the Hunts' former pastor, I have seen them prayerfully wait for their children to arrive and then I've had the opportunity to join in as they joyfully dedicated those children to the Lord.

This book explores the emotions—the hopes, fears, and doubts—associated with adoption, but most of all, it is a story of faith in the God who answers prayers and grants the desires of our hearts.

Jerry Falwell

Preface

If you've picked this book up, chances are you're considering adoption. Good for you! No matter what you've heard, adoption doesn't have to be painful, disturbing, expensive, or a "second-best" alternative. It may be considerably more difficult than adding a child to your family the biological way, but believe me, adoption is worth the time and effort.

Whether you are having difficulty conceiving a biological child or you are thinking of adding another child to your present brood, I've tried to point out some commonsense considerations and some spiritual insights that are often overlooked in typical books about adoption.

When we were diagnosed as "infertile," I immediately ran to our Christian book store for something to read that would guide, comfort, and encourage me. I found nothing, so I hope this book will enlighten and encourage you as you seek God's best—His will for your family.

Angela E. Hunt

I
Did not plant you.
True.
But when
The season is done—
When the alternate
Prayers for sun
And for rain
Are counted—
When the pain
Of weeding
And the pride of
Watching are through—
Then I will hold you
High to heaven.
A shining sheaf
Above the thousand
Seeds grown wild.

Not my planting.
But by heaven,
My harvest—
My child.

—Anonymous

ONE
Why Consider Adoption?

As the alarm clock jarred her into consciousness, she automatically reached to shut it off and then fumbled for the thermometer she kept by the bed. Once her fingers found it, she stuck it in her mouth and, as usual, contemplated how nice it would be to stay in bed and not go to work. She was only working until they had a baby, anyway. After the required three minutes had passed, she removed the thermometer and stumbled to the bathroom to record the morning's "resting temperature" on the chart her gynecologist had given her.

She reentered the bedroom, gave her sleeping husband a playful whack on his behind, and called briskly, "Time to get up, oh thou sluggard." She then padded to the kitchen and poured a glass of cold orange juice, her breakfast. Her Bible and a daily devotional guide lay at the end of the kitchen table and she drew them near. She calmly, routinely read the Scripture appointed by the devotional guide and then proceeded to read the book's daily illustration.

The challenge at the bottom of the page brought her reading to an abrupt halt. The lesson questioned, "What is the biggest difficulty in your life right now?"

"Oh, Lord," she breathed, "You know what it is. Our infertility. You know how long and how hard we have been trying to have a baby. You know how often we have prayed, fasted, and prayed again. You know about the doctors, the books, the advice, and the pressure."

She slowly read the next sentence. "Ask God not to remove that difficulty, but to use it to bring you closer to Him and to others."

"No!" her mind screamed in rebellion. "I can't give up this hope. I can't believe that You would ask this of me. Surely You wouldn't, would You, Lord?"

Surely it wasn't the Lord asking her; it was some professorial theologian who had written an impersonal spiritual platitude for July 13. How dare he! How could some unknown writer ask her to divulge and renounce her heart's desire?

But deep within, she knew there was more to it than that. It was July 13, and her calendar was marked "tests due back from doctor's office." It was the day when she and her husband would possibly know something about why they seemed to be the only couple in the world that couldn't produce babies.

As her husband dropped her off at her office later that morning, he kissed her good-bye and reminded her to call the doctor's office after four o'clock. As the day slowly passed, she glanced at the clock every hour and tried to pray. Thinking of the morning's devotional reading, she murmured a quick compromise: "God, I would rather there be no chance for us to have children than merely a little chance. If I've got to give up having a baby, let me do it completely."

When four o'clock finally arrived, she hesitantly dialed the doctor's number. A nurse put her on hold until the doctor came on the line. He spoke, and she replied automatically as if another person had entered her body to make civil replies and thank the doctor for his time and trouble. She hung up and stared at the telephone for a moment, then called out the door to her boss, "Do you mind if I leave a little early today?" He didn't, so she quickly gathered her belongings and left. By the time she was out the door, she was sobbing.

After arriving home, she dreaded her husband's arrival. How could she tell him? What could she say? When at last she heard his key in the lock, she ran to meet him. One look at his face told her that he too had called the doctor. There was nothing that needed to be said.

As they held each other in comforting closeness, they cried together and quietly buried a dream. She told him about her morning's devotion, and he reminded her that God always knows best. He said he was sorry they would never have a daughter like her; she sobbed that she had wanted a son like him.

As they sat on the edge of their bed and cried together, she suddenly spoke out in furious determination. "I know I was meant to have children. I just know it! God gave me a mother's heart and He wouldn't have done that without a reason."

The knowledge that they would never have biological children fueled their desperate desire to be parents. They had time and love to share, so in the midst of their crisis, they decided to adopt. They knew a little about the difficulties of adoption, the months of waiting, and hours of preparatory paperwork, but they were willing to undergo anything to bring a child into their home.

The above story is ours: Gary and Angie Hunt's. Many months have passed since that July 13, but I can recall those intense feelings vividly. I have prayed that I would not forget all of the emotions we experienced so that I could empathize with others who find themselves incapable of bearing children.

Five years later I was invited to speak to a ladies' conference on the subject of praise. A busy mother of two, a youth pastor's wife, and a full-time writer, I felt in control and on top of the world. I decided my topic would center around praise for God's plan in bringing my children home and I'd be professional, poised, and totally polished.

What a mess I made of my plans! As the gulf breezes blew over our casual breakfast gathering, I took out a journal I kept during the months I waited for my children to come home. As I tried to impassively read the words I had written years before, hot tears ran down my face and my voice alternated between control and tremor.

The ladies to whom I'd hoped to minister reached into their handbags and ministered to me. "Have a tissue," offered one lady, and another woman soothed me, "Take your time. We understand."

I suppose there are some things deep in the soul of a man or woman that can never be shared on the level of a simple illustration. There are some wounds which God heals that can never be reopened without tears, even tears of joy, and there are some struggles through life that are never completely conquered.

As I shared and cried with those women that day, we found we had much in common. Several of them had adopted children of their own. I've heard that you never notice Volkswagens on the road until you own one yourself; similarly, I had never thought about adoption until we announced our plans to adopt. Suddenly, adopted children and adoptive parents surfaced from everywhere. I found that many of my adult friends had been adopted, many families in our church had adopted children, and many people began to quietly take me aside and say, "You know, my wife and I are considering adoption. You see, we can't seem to have a baby and. . . ."

Infertility on the Rise
For many reasons, infertility is on the rise. The American Fertility Society (AFS), based in Birmingham, Alabama, reports that one in six couples of childbearing age today is infertile (unable to conceive a child after one year of unprotected intercourse). The AFS also has found that 40 percent of infertility is attributable to men, 40 percent to women, and 20 percent can't be pegged specifically to either partner. In ten percent of the cases doctors cannot determine the cause of infertility.[1]

There are many medical treatments for infertility which are relatively simple and can be kept very private. A couple who has not conceived after one year should check with their doctor, but keep in mind that it often takes six to eight months for a normal fertile couple to conceive.[2]

There has been much publicity about the more complicated means of artificial conception, i.e., test-tube babies, embryo freezing, surrogate mothering, and artificial insemination. Personally, I believe that conceiving life outside of the body is a great miracle, but we must consider how God could bless such an endeavor when many fertilized eggs are thoughtlessly discarded. When we allow a tiny human life to be thrown away, we have ignored the sanctity of human life. If the "test-tube" procedure could be guaranteed to use only one fertilized egg, and if the egg and sperm were those of the husband and wife, then perhaps this could be a valuable procedure for infertile couples.

In our case, artificial insemination was one option. There are two types: AID (artificial insemination by donor) and AIH (artificial insemination by husband). When the very professional doctor described the AID procedure to us, he remarked that all sperm donors at his particular hospital were "very intelligent medical students mostly," and were free of detectable genetic defects. His description sounded too much like something Hitler would have endorsed, and I did not like the idea of voluntarily choosing to carry another man's child. For us, there were children enough who needed homes through adoption; we were more than willing to reach out to them.

During the 21 months that we tried to conceive, I rode an unbelievable emotional roller coaster. My girlfriends at the office would help me plot my temperature charts and circle days on the calendar. "Call your husband and hurry home on your lunch hour," one woman joked. "Today's the day to make babies!"

In the latter two weeks of my cycle, I would vividly imagine morning sickness and all sorts of pregnancy symptoms, I would eat a huge meal and then look at food and think: "Am I nauseous? Yes—I think so. I must be pregnant!"

Each time my menstruation was delayed for two or three days (which was often because of my agitated state of mind),

I'd confide to my friends that I was 99 percent sure I was pregnant. I bought home pregnancy test kits and I'd dreamily sit at work with one protective hand over my tummy. If I had a cold or hay fever, I'd determinedly suffer and sniff rather than risk taking a drug when there might be a small unannounced baby within my body.

Inevitably, however, the physical reality would manifest itself and my hopes would be abruptly snatched away. For almost two years I vacillated monthly between the heights of hope and the depths of despair.

We found that we had to put the desire for a pregnancy behind us. After all, pregnancy is not all fun and games, so my infatuation with pregnancy passed quickly once we had decided to adopt. I detest nausea, and found that I was even able to joke that "at least I won't have to get fat."

I can't say that I never wonder how it feels to have a baby kick inside the womb. It must be incredible to know that a human life, part of you and part of your loved one, is growing while you warm and nurture it. Pregnant women get congratulations, personal attention, and seats on the bus. They get to wear those wonderful tents with bows on top.

But I wanted a child to love, not a season of maternity tents. Adoption was the right choice for us—and for me.

The Challenge to Find a Child

We thought that adoption would be reasonably easy. After all, aren't there thousands of unwanted children in the world? Unfortunately for the children, there are. According to the U.S. Department of Health and Human Services, in 1984 there were 270,000 children, most of them older, handicapped, or from minority racial backgrounds, tied up in foster care and the number continues to rise each year.[3]

The white healthy infant is the most sought after and least available child. According to the National Committee for Adoption, only 10 percent of women who bear babies out of wedlock made adoption plans for their children, compared with approximately 80 percent a generation ago. Only about 50,000 women place infants for adoption today and abortions take the lives of 1.6 million babies each year.[4]

In the 1960s the Children's Home Society of California had to make televised appeals to recruit parents for all the infants who needed homes. In 1969, CHS placed 2,000 infants. In 1984 only 300 infants were placed and for each of those infants there were 15 waiting parents.[5]

According to William L. Pierce, president of the National Committee for Adoption, in 1985 approximately 25,000 healthy newborns were adopted in the United States through licensed agencies and independent placements. More people are adopting independently today; a typical agency may place between 10 and 20 infants per year and for every available child there are 40 couples who want to adopt (other experts cite as many as 100 couples per child).[6]

There are agencies which are making amazing progress. When Ed and Victoria McMahon were featured on the cover of *People* magazine with their newly adopted infant daughter, the agency featured inside was Arty Elgart's Golden Cradle agency in Philadelphia, Pennsylvania. Unlike most traditional agencies, which wait for pregnant women to come to them, Elgart found success through aggressive advertisement. In 1985 he placed 125 babies—three times more than one of the largest New York agencies.

Elgart's methods are unconventional. Often a biological mother will live with a couple who wishes to adopt (though never the couple which might receive her infant) allowing both mother and adoptive couple to learn about the frustration and pain each feels. The birth mother is assured of her privacy and her medical bills are paid by the adopting couple. The baby will be placed in the arms of the prospective adoptive parents 72 hours after birth. The agency is licensed, nonprofit, and state-approved. The fees are $9,000 for state residents and $11,000 for those in the Golden Cradle's service area but out of Pennsylvania.[7]

Before a couple even begins to evaluate agencies, they should realistically try to visualize their "ideal child." Recently I watched a television talk show on a Christian network. The topic was adoption and the hostess had formed a panel consisting of a social worker, adoptive parent, adopted teenager, and a couple who had been refused by one private agency.

The hostess of the program spent a lot of time sympathizing with the couple who had been refused. The reason? They were in their forties and had been refused an infant. They would consider no other children, and had tried no other agencies. Their limited vision frustrated and angered me. Yet, like them, many people are deliberately cutting themselves off from what God could do in their homes. There are many older children and sibling groups who need homes. Why do people feel they must adopt an infant?

It's obvious that most people want to begin parenting while their child's life is still young, fresh, and virtually untouched. We've all heard that most of a child's personality is formed by age six, so we think, *If we're to have input in a child's life, let's get a young child!* But seven-year-olds need homes too. So do teenagers.

It is true that most agencies prefer to place infants with young couples. However, many agencies would love to place older children with older parents because raising an older child often requires some extra maturity and parenting experience.

If you feel God may be leading you to consider adoption, take time to consider the vast array of children from which you have to choose. Don't limit yourself or your family to one type of child. In later chapters we will be discussing the many options within adoption and the many children who wait for homes.

Begin Adoption Only When You Are Ready
If you are infertile, allow yourself time to grieve before you pursue adoption. I did not realize it at the time, but I actively

grieved for three months after that fateful day of July 13. For weeks one glance at a baby could reduce me to tears. In the midst of a mundane conversation about the water bill I could suddenly burst out with, "It really isn't fair! Why can't we have kids?"

There are stages to grief: depression, anger, denial, despair, bargaining, and finally, acceptance. Acceptance doesn't mean that you're happy with the situation (though, now I can say that I am), but that you have ceased to grieve. I went through some of the stages during the time we tried to conceive. I went through others later. But by the time we faced a social worker and solidified our plans to adopt, we had accepted God's plan for us.

Infertile couples, particularly women, often feel a sort of desperation to have a child. The violent emotions that surface when an infertile woman must contend with pregnant friends, baby showers, and small children are not easily subdued. Often feelings of inferiority and inadequacy arise that may put a strain on the marriage and on other relationships. Many infertile women describe themselves as "empty," "worthless," or "hopeless." The Bible records the desperation of Hannah, who prayed for a child so fervently that the priest thought she was drunk, and Rachel, who passionately told her husband, "Give me children or I'll die!" (Gen. 30:1, NIV)

If you've had to deal with the struggles of infertility, wait until your emotions have calmed before you meet a social worker and begin your adoption inquiries. You need to be under control and emotionally stable—no social worker will want to place a child with a woman who sobs at the sight of a box of Pampers.

The devotional I read that July morning said to "allow the difficulty to draw you closer to God and to others." Infertility must be shared; it cannot be blamed on one person or the other. As you believe that God has brought you and your spouse together, you must believe that He has allowed this difficulty in His wisdom.

It will be helpful if you can share your emotions regarding

infertility. You must find trustworthy people, however, and many infertile couples are unwilling to discuss their situation with others. They are afraid they will be offered mundane advice or their trouble will be considered too lightly.

One support group for infertile couples is Resolve, Inc. This organization provides telephone counseling, medical information, and educational programs. Resolve support chapters have been formed throughout the country.[8]

It is true that infertile couples with no children are usually the first choice of adoption agencies for infants. But perhaps you are experiencing secondary infertility—you have one child, but cannot seem to have a second. Again, check with your doctor. If there is an incorrectible medical problem, check with an adoption agency. You have one valuable asset: parenting experience! You may be the perfect parents for a preschooler or a family of five siblings. Check with the various agencies in your area to see how you would be regarded.

Perhaps you are not infertile, but concerned about social causes and would like to adopt to help a neglected child or to inhibit the population growth. Perhaps you are single, but you feel you could provide a home for kids. To be honest, you would not be a first choice on most agencies' lists, unless you were willing and able to handle a "hard to place" child (a child with a disability or handicap, a racially mixed child, an older child, or a sibling group).

Jim Forderer, a bachelor from San Jose, California, has adopted a family of six boys. One of them was emotionally disturbed and the rest were physically handicapped. Forderer said, "I didn't look for healthy children. In my case, these kids were not a last resort. They were my first choice."[9]

In July 1985, *McCall's* magazine reported on the home of Keith and Sharon Grill. The Grills have 14 children—seven biological, six adopted, and one foster child. Of these, seven have health problems, ranging from spina bifida to Down's syndrome. Of her family, Sharon says, "Some people play tennis or racquetball. This is what I do."[10]

Just remember that children are children, no matter what

their bodies are like, what color their skin is, or where they have come from. All children need permanency and consistency, and no matter what your situation, if you can provide those things, there will be an agency willing to talk to you about adopting one of their waiting children.

If you want to adopt a child to provide a playmate for your biological children or to replace a child you have lost through death or divorce, think again. Children deserve to be adopted for who they are as individuals, not because of any other child's influence or role. Any good social worker will try to discern why parents want to adopt, and they will be considering the child's best interests.

Consider God's Call for Your Life
While you are pondering your reasons for adoption and parenthood, perhaps you should consider that God may intend for you to remain childless. My husband and I know, without question, that we were meant to be parents. Like a bird was meant to fly, I was meant to mother. I have no doubts.

Recently I had the opportunity to interview Rexella Van Impe, wife of the well-known evangelist Jack Van Impe. This couple has dedicated their marriage to Christian service and God saw fit to keep them childless. Rexella is a beautiful woman. When we met I was battling a cold I had picked up from my kids and with my red nose, scratchy voice, and antihistamine-fogged brain, I felt like the pauper next to a princess.

Rexella was immaculately dressed in an off-white suit; her gold jewelry provided accents in just the right places. Her makeup was perfect, not an excess or a smear anywhere, and her gestures were straight out of the charm school text I wish I'd studied.

When I asked Dr. and Mrs. Van Impe if they had children, there was an awkward silence. Dr. Van Impe shook his head no. "We have a cat, Finaca," he joked.

I would have ignored the silence and moved on, but Rexella

stopped. "Could I add something about having children?" she asked quietly. I nodded.

"There are some women who are going to perk up their hearts when they read this. It is not God's will," she paused and spoke slowly, "that I have children. He had something different for me. What could be better than having a family? I was just like any other woman; that was my first goal in life practically right after we were married. Normality says this— that we women were created to have children."

She leaned forward and continued earnestly. "There's only one thing better than having the normal thing, and that's having God's will for your life. I could never get up from my knees after *begging* for children until I put that as a tag on the end of my prayer: 'But God, more than anything I want your will.' So He gave me His will, and that was to be childless and barren as far as the physical, but He's given to us thousands upon thousands of spiritual children. That was the better thing for our house."

"I have women writing to me all the time and asking me about this. They say, 'I'm going to have a nervous breakdown—I've got to have some children.' So the Lord has allowed me, because of my own experience, to comfort those hearts and to help them through a very troublesome time."

I told Rexella I appreciated her comments; I too had wrestled with the desire for children, but my husband and I had decided to adopt.

"Adoption is a wonderful thing," she quickly added. "This idea came to us also and we prayed so much about it. To most girls who write to us with this problem, I say, 'Do investigate adoption because God may have that perfect baby for you out there.' But then again, the Lord said no to us because He had something different for us."[11]

Through infertility you may find that adoption is a higher calling, a larger challenge to call upon God's grace. You may decide to meet the challenge medically or through foster parenting. Like Rexella Van Impe, you may learn that you are to be a spiritual parent alone. No matter how infertility is viewed, it is a condition which strikes at the deepest heart of those who experience it. But you and your spouse can face anything God allows if you face it together.

After much prayer, if you feel that God has called you and your mate to be parents, the decision to adopt is usually not hard to make. It is only the first of many major decisions that will present themselves to you, so seek guidance and help from the Lord every step of the way. Adoption will change your life and the lives of those closest to you, so be sure you are following the Lord's leading.

TWO
Where Are the Children?

Once you have made the decision to adopt, your next step is frustratingly simple: to find a child. Most adoptions are arranged through agencies; adoptions without agencies are called independent adoptions.

Independent Adoptions
Independent adoptions are usually arranged through a doctor or lawyer who knows of a situation in which a baby is going to be placed for adoption. The lawyer contacts the prospective adoptive parents, and usually they arrange to pay for certain medical bills and legal expenses. They may even pay to have the biological mother live in another area for the last few months of her pregnancy. The lawyer usually exacts a hefty fee, and possibly the doctor will also, if he has arranged the adoption.

Independent adoptions are risky, for the biological mother may change her mind and keep the baby after the adoptive parents have spent thousands of dollars for her care. Six states have declared independent adoptions illegal: in North Dakota, Michigan, Delaware, and Minnesota the practice is forbidden; in Connecticut and Massachusetts parents may locate a birth mother independently, but then state agencies and social workers must oversee the entire situation and make sure that everything is done in accordance with the law.[1]

Recently a newspaper carried the shocking story of an adoption scam. A couple who had desperately sought a baby through infertility procedures finally contacted an adoption lawyer who knew of another couple wishing to place an infant for adoption.

The two couples met face to face, arranged the independent adoption, and finalized the financial arrangements. The adoptive couple agreed to spend about $4,000 including attorney's fees and charitable contributions for the birth mother. The baby was yet unborn, but was due in two months.

The birth mother needed clothes and money for a place to stay, so the adoptive couple rushed to provide $1,550.00 and bought the girl and her boyfriend a telephone and a heater for their apartment.

Two weeks before the baby was due the birth mother called in a panic. She was at the hospital, experiencing contractions, and the ultrasound test showed a fully-developed six-pound boy. The adoptive couple was thrilled and they plunged into preparation.

Then the birth mother disappeared. Someone began an investigation and discovered that the birth mother had promised nine children and received over $11,000 from seven couples. Authorities doubt that she was even pregnant. No one bothered to check.[2]

In Texas, the state which leads the nation in adoptions, biological mothers may place their babies directly with minimal regulation. The laws have been misused and need to be tightened. "We know that women get cars to give up their babies, or shopping sprees or college scholarships," said Jeff Rosenberg of the National Committee for Adoption. "There are a lot of lawyers out there doing private adoptions. Some of them make a very good living."[3]

In 1986 a Dallas lawyer was convicted of buying a child. The mother testified that the lawyer paid her more than $2,000 for rent, groceries, maternity clothes, and taxi fares during her pregnancy. (State law restricts payments to mothers to necessary medical or legal expenses.) A New York woman testified that she and her husband paid the lawyer $14,000 for adopting the child, a procedure they believed to be legal. The lawyer was sentenced to seven years in prison.[4]

If the adoption occurs between a biological mother and adoptive parents without any intermediary, the confidentiality of the biological mother and adoptive parents cannot be maintained. Independent adoptions often smack of "baby selling," and thus this area is sometimes called "gray market adoption." Of course, many babies are successfully adopted through this method, but I would not recommend it.[5]

Agency Adoptions

Agency adoptions, on the other hand, are usually very safe. Social workers do their utmost to protect the anonymity of all involved parties and they are experts on the adoption laws in their respective states. There are basically two types of agencies, public and private.

Public Agencies. Public agencies are run by respective state governments and usually place children only within their state. Children who are available to these agencies often have been removed from their homes by the court due to parental neglect or abandonment. The court often places infants, whose biological mothers choose adoption after counseling, with a city or state social worker. Rarely do agencies place orphans. In the unusual case of both parents dying, children are usually placed with the nearest relative who is willing to care for the child.

Public agencies usually do not charge a fee because tax dollars are the source of funds for these agencies. The only expenses you will incur involve those of an attorney when the adoption is petitioned (finalized) in court. Public agencies' requirements are not stringent; however, the home study will thoroughly interpret your personality, home environment, and background. Logically, most public agencies prefer couples who have been married for at least one year and are over the age of 18.

Public agencies have no requirements regarding race, religion, family size, or income. Because they receive a great diversity of children, they know that many types of homes are good prospects for their children. Public agencies very often place older children, minority children, and sibling groups.

It is important for prospective parents to know how placements occur in the public agency. Many parents feel that once their home study is completed, they are simply placed on the bottom of "the list," and as names are scratched off the top, their name automatically rises until the next child available is offered to them. It is not this simple.

A printed copy of your home study, your complete "life story," is copied and sent to the central state office. When a child becomes available, his or her report is also sent to the central office. This is where prospective parents and children are matched. The central office will put the parents' social worker and the child's social worker in touch with each other and the adoption will be well underway.

Periodically, the social workers from many cities may meet to discuss new children who have come into care. Biographies of the children will be exchanged and social workers will search through the many home study reports to find a family that will suit the child. Although parents who have been waiting for some time might have some priority, what the social workers try to do is find the best home for the child. Many factors enter into this: the child's age, history, learning abilities and disabilities, and temperament. They also consider a family's age, parenting experience, stability, lifestyle, marital relationship, and personality make-up. Considering all the factors that must be evaluated when matching parents and children together for life, you begin to see the tremendous task social workers face.

When the social worker has found a family for a child or set of children, the family will be given a call. If the child is older, the worker may suggest several meetings in advance for the family and child to meet and "size each other up." The family may be shown a video of the child. A private meeting will be arranged with the prospective adoptive parents where they will be told as much as is known about the child's background, genetic history, and reason placed for adoption. Depending on the circumstances, the social worker may or may not tell who the child's biological parents are, but those parents will not know who the adoptive parents are. Confidentiality is guaranteed by the courts for most adoptions.

If the parents accept the child, the child is taken home. In each state, there is a trial period in which the adoptive parents raise the child but the adoption is not yet finalized. Technically, the guardianship of the child rests with the placing agency until the trial period has passed and the adoption is finalized by the court, but emotionally, that child is already a part of the new family.

There is a category of adoption known as "legal risk." This means that the child has been allowed to live with the prospective adoptive parents before his or her birth parents have relinquished parental rights. The adoptive parents, who really are foster parents at this point, are at legal risk of losing the child. I know one couple who had a "legal risk" adoption. Their daughter, whom they loved dearly, had not been relinquished by her birth parents. The situation was strained and very difficult. Proceed with caution into a "legal risk" involvement.

Private Agencies. If you do not choose a public adoption agency, you may investigate private, nonprofit adoption agencies which usually are self-supporting or supported in part by contributions, by a church, or by some other charitable organization. Some agencies also receive government funds to provide services for children who are in the care of the state. Private agencies can charge various fees and develop their own requirements for prospective adoptive parents. However, state licensing laws for these agencies may prescribe fee ceilings and other special criteria.

When we first began to pursue adoption, I called the public agency in our town (usually listed under the Social Welfare or Service in the telephone directory), and I also checked with many private agencies. There were a couple of private agencies listed in our phone book, and I also found several agencies listed in books about adoption at our local library.[6]

Private agencies do their own home studies in accordance with state laws and oversee all the legalities of adoption without help from public sources. Therefore, a private agency located in a neighboring state may be willing to handle your adoption, but you will have to travel to the agency several times for home study interviews, and at least once someone from the agency will have to come to your home. Often private agencies' long waiting lists from within their own state do not permit them to accept out-of-state applications. Or they may accept your application and merely file it. Don't waste your time with such an agency. There are too many others who could help you.

If possible, find an agency within your state. Each state has different laws regarding adoption, and you must adhere to the laws of the state in which you reside. An agency in the same state will be better equipped to help you, and being geographically closer is a big advantage.

How do private agencies operate? How do they receive custody of the children they place?

Most private agencies place children who have been entrusted to them at birth or through legal action. For example, one church I used to attend operates a home for unwed mothers and an adoption agency. Girls who come to the home are given, unpressured, the choice of whether to raise their babies themselves or make an adoption plan. Those who choose adoption sign custody papers placing their babies with the agency; they can be sure that their babies will be placed into homes carefully screened by the ministry. Custody is not transferred to the adoptive parents until the trial period is over and the adoption is finalized by the courts.

Private agencies can develop their own particular requirements in accordance with their philosophies. For instance, most religious agencies have sectarian requirements. Often they will place children only into families of their particular denomination. Usually there are minimum and maximum age requirements, health requirements, and generally such agencies give preferential status to infertile couples that have no other children. Some agencies require that the adoptive mother either not work or take at least a six-week maternity leave after the child arrives. Each private agency is different, so be sure to check on the individual requirements.

Private agencies also differ a great deal in financial arrangements. The fee you pay supports the agency and its staff. Often the agency pays for much of the biological mother's medical treatment expenses. Agencies therefore try to be fair and set a common fee for all prospective parents. Many agencies, particularly religious, nonprofit organizations, operate on a sliding scale. I have seen sliding scale fee requirements ranging from 7 percent to 15 percent of a couple's gross combined annual income. Usually part of the fee is submitted with the application, part upon completion of the home study, and the rest is due upon the arrival of the child. Application fees range from $25 to $1,500, so choose an agency carefully before you submit your application.

It is often considered unethical to be on the waiting list of more than one agency at one time, so if you are making no progress with one agency, you may withdraw your name and begin with another. But remember that you may have to go through the entire home-study process again with another agency. Choose an agency with care, and be prepared to wait it out.

Rejection
What if you are rejected by an adoption agency? Most agencies will tell you on the phone if you do not meet their require-

ments for adoptive parents, but if you find that you are rejected after the home study, you may try another agency. But
carefully analyze why the rejection occurred. Are you considered too old for an infant? Then consider an older child. Is
your marriage on rocky ground? A child would only worsen the
situation, so work on your marriage first. Was there an instant
"personality clash" between you and your social worker? If so,
try another agency. Don't feel that social workers are venge-
fully "playing God," but realize they are first concerned with
the welfare of the children they represent.

I was so anxious to begin the adoption procedure that I was
on the phone every day for a month, calling every agency I
could find. I called "information" in every large city near us
(and some not so near), and asked for the information opera-
tor's supervisor. The supervisor would check that city's yellow
pages under "adoption agencies," so I quickly filled a yellow
legal pad with various names and phone numbers. Finally, after
many calls, questions, and frustrations, we narrowed our options. We chose our city's public agency.

You do not have to begin in such a haphazard fashion. Go to
your local public library and look at its collection of telephone
directories for listings. Also, check the Agency Listings on
page 142. Begin with the agencies nearest you.

Practical Considerations for Choosing an Agency
What questions should you ask as you choose an agency?
Here's a checklist to give you ideas:

1. What types of children are available through this
agency? Ask about age, nationalities, and handicaps. Do
they place children out of state? Do they handle international adoptions?
2. Are there any restrictions on who can apply to adopt
through this agency such as age, income, length of marriage, previous divorce, single parent, or religion? What

kinds of families are needed? Do the restrictions vary
with different programs or types of children?

3. How many children did this agency place last year?
What types of children were these? How many applications did the agency accept last year?

4. How is the adoption home study done? What are the
prospective parents' roles in the process? The worker's
role? The agency's role? How soon after application will
the home study begin? How long will it take to complete?
When will we know if we have been approved? If we are
not approved, can we find out why?

5. How long will it take from home study approval to
referral of a child? What happens if we do not feel that we
can accept the child offered to us?

6. What are the unique features of the agency? Are the
office, the staff, and the social workers easily accessible?
Is it possible to talk with families who have adopted
through the agency and through the programs in which
we are interested? Is the agency public or private?

7. What are the costs involved and how are they handled? What extra charges (travel, telephone, other fees)
might we expect? Does the adoption fee cover the home
study, all post-placement visits, the fee to the placing
agency, international processing, transportation, docu-
ment preparations, notarization, medical exams, transla-
tions, visa, etc.?

8. Are the foreign agencies you work with licensed in
their own countries?

9. What kind of support services to families and children
do you offer before, during, after placement, and after
finalization?

10. What if the adoption does not work out?[7]

When I first called our city's social worker, I was immediately impressed by her cheerful, optimistic voice. Prospective
adoptive parents need megadoses of optimism every week or
so. I quickly jotted down the date she mentioned for the

monthly "informational meeting."

Nothing short of the Second Coming could have kept us from that meeting. Gary and I were so excited that both of us actually shook with nervous energy. We couldn't help wondering—were we dressed right? Did we look mature and under control? I prayed, "Lord, please help me keep my emotions calm. I just can't cry here." I'm one of those people who never knows when the flood-dam is going to spring a leak and babies were still a sensitive issue with me.

After finding the Social Services Department and wandering through the halls in the old building, we were shown into a small room with two worn couches and a coffee table. One small attempt at decoration, a calendar with a grinning monkey pictured on it, hung on the back of the oft-painted door. One other couple wandered in, as hopeful and as anxious as we were.

We began to chat and found that they also attended our church. I was relieved. I had to admit that I had some reservations about how a Christian would be perceived in a secular, public agency. Somehow I felt that a public agency social worker might feel that I was too fanatic, or that my youth pastor husband was too religious to be a good parent. It seemed that our local newspaper had a story about a "fundamentalist Christian sect" beating children every day. If I were to mention that I believed in spanking children, would the social worker assume I was a child-beater?

My fears were allayed, however, when the couple with us mentioned that several other couples in our church had adopted children through this agency, and with the help of a particular social worker, Helen.

Helen breezed into the room looking undaunted and optimistic as she had sounded on the phone. She briefly told us about public agency adoptions and what we could expect in the home study when we were ready to begin. She gave each of us an application with the instruction to "mail it in whenever you're ready to begin, and I'll set up the first home study appointment."

If I had been confident enough to ask her to wait half an hour, I would have handed her our completed application on the spot; we were so eager. But we took it home, filled it out immediately, and had it in the mail the next day.

So began the 18 months of waiting that we endured before our miracle occurred. One morning the phone rang at 5 a.m. Gary sleepily staggered up to answer it, and after listening briefly to make sure no one had died, I was just about to go back to sleep when Gary said, "Honey, you take it. It's Joe."

Joe Hale, our friend from college who was currently a missionary in Korea? Joe was calling us? I thought I was still asleep.

"Angie?" Joe's voice hummed over the line. "Listen, I can't talk long, but we've got this three-month-old baby girl my neighbor found on a doorstep. Do you want to see if you can adopt her?"

Did I! I told Joe we'd check on the procedure, then hung up and went back to bed. As I tried to sleep and temper my rising hopes, I wondered why the Lord would choose to bring a baby into our lives on that day and not six months before. "Lord, is this our baby?" I asked aloud.

The International Adoption Agency

To handle this baby's adoption, we encountered another type of private agency: the international adoption agency. International adoptions are handled by only a few agencies (some agencies handle both international and domestic placements), but since so few infants are being placed in this country, more people are checking into international adoption.

I had heard of the Holt Agency, a Christian agency located in Eugene, Oregon. Holt was founded many years ago by Harry Holt, who pioneered adoptions from South Korea. I was impressed with their organization, but at the time they did not have a branch office in our state. We had to find an international agency that could work with us.

The requirements for international adoptions vary, depending on the country of the child's origin. Each country stipulates different conditions for adoptive parents, so you must check carefully to see the countries for which you are eligible. International adoptions are usually, but not always, more expensive than domestic adoptions. The legitimate expenses include fees for: both the foreign and the U.S. adoption agencies, the air fare, the home study, travel expenses in this country, and miscellaneous ones to the Immigration and Naturalization Service (INS). When we picked up our new daughter at the Washington National Airport, we found that most of the adoptive parents in our group had two things in common: new children and new second mortgages!

Adoption agencies are now springing up to handle adoptions from South American countries where so many children have been recently orphaned. INS has published a new booklet to help provide information about intercountry adoption: *The Immigration of Adopted and Prospective Adoptive Children.*[8]

Let me stress that your adoption procedures will doubtless be very different from ours. Each agency—public and private—is different, with its own regulations and rules, and each state has its own set of adoption laws.[9] Although you may travel a different road to your goal, the end result will be quite similar. There is nothing quite like welcoming a new child into a loving home.

THREE
How an Adoption Is Begun: The Home Study

Nothing is quite so delightful or as nerve-wracking as the adoption home study. Adoptive parents are usually eager to begin, for nothing can be done until the study is finished; yet they dread the prospect of having their home, marriage, and background under the social worker's probing gaze.

When does the home study begin? This will depend upon the agency you select. Some agencies will begin a home study immediately, file your records, and console you as you begin your serious waiting. Many other agencies, who have back-logged applications and few children, may require interested parents to delay the home study until other waiting parents receive children. This leaves the pre-home study parents free to change agencies if they wish. I recommend that you choose an agency which can begin your home study as soon as possible.

Who conducts the home study? Usually just one social worker from the agency you've registered with will be assigned to conduct your home study. You won't face a barrage of inquisitors. You'll just talk with one social worker who will usually be a female.

Where will the home study be conducted? Anywhere you like. At least one meeting must be held in your home (be prepared to give a guided tour of the place), but the other meetings could be held at the agency office.

How should you act during the home study? As naturally as possible. Your social worker should know the concerns and anxieties of adoptive couples, so she'll be able to spot phoniness in a flash. Just be yourself, and don't be afraid to express your reservations, frustrations, or questions.

Now that we've established the who, when, where, and how, exactly *what* is the home study? Exactly what its name implies: a study of your home. Its purpose is twofold: to make sure that your home environment is suitable for raising a child, and to evaluate what type of child would easily fit into your family's "temperament."

Have you ever considered how many types of families there are? We all know proper families, bookish families, athletic families, close-knit families, and outgoing families. Even if your family consists only of you and your spouse, you have a certain "family personality" which will be evident to your social worker. One friend of mine has two adopted children and two biological. Her "bio" children, like her and her husband, are indoor types. They've found it a challenge to integrate two "outdoor, playground-loving kids" into their family.

The home study will evaluate your individual personalities, family personality, marriage, lifestyle, extended family relationships, financial situation, purpose for living, and your personal and inter-personal goals. In short, everything about you could be scrutinized.

How is this done? Gary and I found the whole process really to be painless and quite cathartic. In fact, during our subsequent adoption when our old home study was reevaluated and "updated" by new social workers, we looked forward to the opportunity of sharing our family's history and the story of how God had miraculously worked to bring us together. Our second home study was a variation on the first—a home visit, a time of watching Taryn interact with us, and a question/answer session about requirements and regulations, with a mutual "let's-size-each-other-up" feeling.

Our first social worker, Helen, arranged our home study into six meetings—one meeting each week for six weeks. We began on September 16 at lunchtime. Gary and I took long lunch breaks from work for these special occasions.

The purpose of our first meeting was very basic. Helen wanted to know a little about us and why we wanted to adopt. It was a "get acquainted and get comfortable" meeting. We talked casually, and Gary and Helen veered off into a conversation about racquetball that left me out in the cold. But the meeting accomplished its purpose—we were acquainted. Before we left, Helen pulled out her pocket calendar, considered it carefully, and set the date for the next meeting. Eager as always, I suggested the required "home visit" for our next get-together. She agreed, and we set the date for September 21, just five days later. I was thrilled—the sooner, the better.

I tried not to clean the house too much because I wanted to let it look lived in, but I did vacuum under the beds and banish our cats to the basement so that my Angora's long white hairs wouldn't cover Helen's clothes.

Helen arrived a fashionable ten minutes late and informed us that this session was to cover either Gary or me in depth. I was elected and Gary retreated to the backyard while I gave Helen the house tour. She didn't pull a white glove inspection, she just walked through and complimented me on various arrangements and pictures.

We then sat down to chat. I felt a little like I was in a psychiatrist's office as I responded to her questions. I remember her asking, "Do your sisters like you?" and "How does your mother feel about you?" We talked about my family, my background, and just plain history—what I did after high school, after college, and jobs I had held. She looked at family photo albums and photographs on the wall. I felt she was getting a very good picture of how my parents and family actually looked and acted. All the while she spoke, she took notes on a yellow legal pad. I tried peeking over her shoulder once, but found that her shorthand writing could not be deciphered. So much for my nosiness, but I was dying to see what she was saying about us.

Our next home study, held at Helen's office, was September 30. Helen brought her brown-bag lunch and herbal tea; Gary and I brought a bag from Hardees. This time Gary was under scrutiny. He talked about his family, good and bad, his mother's fight with cancer, and her death three years before. He answered questions about his sister, his brother-in-law, and his niece and nephew. They discussed his grandparents, aunts and uncles, and cousins. I enjoyed listening to the whole conversation because unknown parts of my husband's history were opening up to me.

Before we left, Helen consulted her calendar and asked if we could meet again on October 6 at noon. "Of course!" I exclaimed. I would have done anything to make room in our schedules for those meetings.

During our fourth meeting we discussed our marriage and personal goals. Gary and I talked about our jobs, but mentioned that I was planning to quit working outside the home once we received a child. Helen was very interested in the problems of adjustment we experienced during our first year of marriage; I suppose she was analyzing our ability to cope with new situations. I thought it odd, but we never really talked about children or philosophies of child-rearing. Helen was more interested in us as we were than in what we would be with children.

The next three weeks were frustrating because first Helen was out of town; then we were away on a business trip. We weren't able to meet for three weeks, but finally we set a date of November 2 and met around the lunch table as usual.

Helen warned us that this meeting would be difficult, and it was. We finally brought up the unmentioned subject of children. Helen wanted us to tell her what children we would find acceptable and what situations we would find unacceptable.

We were so desperate for a child that we felt we would take anything. It's hard for emotionally hyped parents to be realistic, but we were able to set some guidelines.

Age? Because we had no parenting experience and because

we were young, we decided to request preschool or younger. We knew that there were very few infants available and thought our willingness to accept an older child might speed the adoption process. Indeed, many agencies will tell you that the speed of your adoption will depend a great deal on how "flexible" you are in the choice of your child's age.

Sex? We really didn't care. It was easy to be impartial on this consideration for us, but it is a fact that girls are more often requested than boys. Though no one could prove why this is true, some psychologists believe that men can accept an adoptive daughter more easily than an adopted son. The masculine pride that touts sonship and "carrying on the family name" is still strong in American families and even stronger in other foreign cultures where any type of adoption is rare.

After these two criteria were settled, things became more difficult. Race? Social workers infrequently place black children in white families, but what about biracial children? Personally we didn't have any problem with accepting a biracial child, but we wondered how the child would fit into our home and the southern society which surrounded us. I don't believe, however, that a biracial child would have been offered to us because there are mixed-race couples to adopt these children.

What about an abused child? What about a child whose mother was mentally ill? A child who was a product of rape? How about a child with a learning disability? There are many types of problem children, consider a child with:

—low birth weight?
—premature birth?
—visible birthmark?
—major or minor heart defects?
—a child needing a sex change?
—a child with a missing limb?
—cerebral palsy?
—malformations of fingers or toes?
—blindness?
—hearing impairment or total deafness?

—diabetes?
—epilepsy?
—a cleft lip and/or palate?
—malnutrition?
—drug dependence since birth?
—developmental delay?
—hyperactivity?
—speech problems?
—dwarfism?

On and on the questions went. Some things were important considerations for us, some mattered not at all. Helen asked about everything from major problems to minor personality flaws: "Would you consider a child who whines?"

We longed so much for a child, any child, that it was difficult to be forced to limit our choices. But it was necessary. Not every child will be perfect for any family. It is easier to verbalize your feelings in hypothetical situations than to recall the social worker because your home is unsuitable for the child placed there.

We tried to see ourselves realistically. Parenting a "normal" child is difficult enough, but parenting a child with special needs requires extra energy and commitment. Do not allow your sense of Christian compassion to lead you into an area for which you are not qualified.

Home with a cold, I was too sick to go to work the day of our final adoption home study meeting, but nothing short of hospitalization would have kept me away from Helen's office. For this meeting Helen asked us to bring five candid photographs of ourselves and a copy of our marriage license. These were necessary for our final home study report. I also brought Helen a beautiful plant for her office "just because we want you to remember us." We had enjoyed our meetings, and I really felt I'd miss these heart-to-heart sessions.

Helen gathered the information we had brought and invited us up to her office. There she brought out her book of available children and we looked at each picture. Of course she knew that we would not find a child just by looking through her book, but she wanted us to see what kind of children were waiting.

Before we left, she told us to feel free to call once a month or so to keep in touch and see how things were going. "I try not to call my waiting parents," she said, "because they nearly have heart failure when they hear my voice. I probably won't call you unless I have good news for you."

She explained that she would prepare a written report on our family from the notes she'd taken and the impressions she had received. That report would be filed in the state office in Richmond and would hopefully be matched with the report on a waiting child.

We were finished. We had done all that we could aggressively do. From that point, all we could passively do was wait and pray.

FOUR
What Kind of Child for You?

Probably the most difficult part of your home study will be learning about the many types of children available. You may feel that you ought to want to provide a home for all of them, but that is not practically possible. During our last home study visit, when our social worker let us look through her "catalog" of available children, we saw many pages, each displaying the picture of a lovely child. Printed alongside the photograph was the biological, social, physical, and mental history of the child in abbreviated form. Most of the children were older, many were part of a sibling group, and many were black or biracial.

Every other month I receive a copy of *Ours* magazine and the first pages I turn to are those where the "waiting children" are featured. I find a particularly appealing face and shamelessly leave the magazine open where my husband will see it— fortunately, though I'd love to take them all, my husband has enough common sense to know what we can and cannot handle!

I recently read the story of Lori Kellog, an adoptive mother of three Korean girls and the founder of Universal Aid for Children, Inc., a child-placing agency in Miami, Florida. Kellog was receiving pictures of orphans and adopting them until finally she had to ask that no more pictures be sent. "The heart was big enough," she said, "but the pocketbook wouldn't make it."[1]

Recently I attended a camp for junior-highers with my husband. A group from a boys' home had joined our church kids, and we were delighted for the chance to work with them. One young boy, obviously fascinated with our daughter, Taryn, came up and asked, "How long have you had her?" I told him and he shyly replied, "I'm up for adoption."

I was startled. "You're what?"

"I'm up for adoption. My foster parents are trying to adopt me."

This sweet boy had lived with his present foster parents for three years and was only now available for adoption. I felt like saying, "Well, if that doesn't work out, you call me. I'll adopt you."

Many people who have adopted fall in love with the experience, but practicality prevails. We simply can't adopt all the children who wait. But others can.

Waiting Older Children

Why do so many older children still wait? Most typical adoptive couples are afraid of what might have happened in the child's past. They fear that some trauma or abuse during the first part of the child's life will not be overcome. The preference is to adopt an infant or a young child with virtually no past history; the adoptive parents want to be the force that shapes and molds the child's personality. This feeling is understandable; it is how my husband and I felt. Gary and I were open to any child under preschool age. Somehow, with no previous parenting experience, we felt safer with a baby or a younger child.

Although no child can be protected from the trauma of separation in an adoption, it is possible that older children can cope with this crisis even better than younger children. A study of 95 families who had adopted children ages 5-12 found that, once the adjustment was over, the age of the child when he was placed made no difference in the outcome of the adoption.[2] Sula Wolff, a recognized authority on the impact of stress on children says:

> All children who need to be looked after outside their own homes, for whatever reason, are children at risk. The people who adopt them are in a unique position to prevent life crises from becoming pathogenic, to prevent separation experiences from developing into deprivation, to provide the kind of upbringing for each child that will make good his past deficiencies.[3]

Many adoptive parents wonder if they will be able to love an older child whose past, personality, and traits are so different from their own. Claudia L. Jewett, the mother of three biological children and seven adopted children writes:

> My own experience with our family totally convinces me that in time it makes no difference how old the child was when he arrived, or whether the child came from my body or from an agency. The love I feel for the children who came to us at thirteen, fourteen, and seventeen is in no way less strong than the love I feel for the children who came to us at the younger ages of two, five, ten, and eleven. The love I feel for our adopted children is in no way less strong than the love I feel for the three children in our family who were born to us. It just doesn't make any difference. It is the caring and sharing that count— love is not prevented by the things and the time that you haven't shared.[4]

Each fall, the New York City Human Resources Administration presents a slide show for potential parents. More than 100 families attend the affair, usually held at Columbia University. The Human Resources Administration is attempting to find homes for older children who have been in foster care for years. Their faces flash across the screen while the narrator reads:

Bruce is 15, and wants to work for a computer company.
Yvette is 11, doesn't like school, but does like boys.
Michael is almost four but cannot talk.
Shavine, 11, offers a line of a poem she wrote: "Waiting
for Spring is an impossible thing."

Waiting for Spring and a forever family is not easy for these
children. They are old enough to understand that they need a
home, that people are considering—and rejecting them—and
that soon, unless someone calls, they will become too old to
be adopted. They will not ever know the blessed security of a
forever family. Many times reports on these children state
simply, "Jose has watched his friends go to adoptive homes
and wonders why he is not chosen. He wants to be adopted
very soon."

In a recent issue of *Parents* I found an article about a couple
who had adopted a nine-year-old girl. "We Have a Problem,"
the article was titled, and in bold print the adoptive mother
wondered, "We felt sure we had enough love and 'people
skills' to carry [the adoption] off. How could we have been so
wrong?"[5]

After reading the article I saw a story of a family who simply
had trouble dealing with the stages of the child's grieving process. After several months of much love and concern, and
careful counseling, the child began to feel "more like Tammy
Mitchell and a little less like the little girl that nobody could
love." The adoption of older children can work.

Sibling Groups

Another category of hard-to-place children is sibling groups.
Couples who would like an "instant family" or people with
families so large that a few more won't make much difference
often consider sibling groups.

Mrs. Roberta Lee Jolly is the mother of such a family. She
and her husband had five children, ages 13 to 19, and were

rearing two grandchildren when they heard about a Chicago priest's aggressive adoption program for black children waiting in foster care. As the Jollys looked through a book of photographs of children needing homes, Mrs. Jolly noticed a photograph of five siblings with the notation: "Adopt out even if separated."

She immediately said to her husband: "Let's not let these children be separated. They've already lost their parents, and now they might lose each other. We must keep them together." And that, according to *Ebony,* is how the Jolly household grew from 9 to 14.[6]

Understandably, adoption agencies usually are not willing to separate biological brothers and sisters, and will not do so unless the adoptive parents are willing for the siblings to keep in touch in the future. As we looked through Helen's notebook of children, I remember two darling girls, ages five and seven, who had to be adopted together and the adoptive parents had to be willing for them to visit their three-year-old sister who had previously been adopted by another family.

Studies have shown that children who are deprived of parents often form a "sub-family" with one child assuming responsibility for the others. In time, the ties between these siblings becomes stronger than the previous ties with the biological parents. When these children are placed together in a temporary foster home, they cling to each other and the ties become even stronger. We all know how much more reassuring it is to enter a strange place with someone we know than alone.

Children who are separated from their brothers or sisters may never overcome their feelings of loss. Such adoptees are more eager to search for their biological families when they are older.

There are advantages to adopting a sibling group. First, the children will be more comfortable and secure with a brother or sister. Second, they can keep each other company, and the older child can help with the younger ones. An older child may be able to understand why the younger child is upset when you are still too unfamiliar with the child's needs and desires.

Third, if you're going to experience all of the emotional hype and preparation in receiving a child, you may find it's easier to receive more than one at once. You'll have an instant family, with the instant problems, but the pleasures that only two or more children can bring.

Some parents may hesitate to adopt siblings because they fear the children will cling to each other and exclude the parents from their affections. This is usually not so. Children, whether adopted or biological, will compete for the parents' attention and affection. Of course they will love each other, but this is much different than the love between parents and children.

Minority Race Children

While many white families would not hesitate to adopt a child of another race, there is a movement among social workers to avoid placing black children in white homes. "We strongly believe blacks should adopt black children and, if provided an opportunity to do so, they will," says Dr. Morris Jeff, president of the National Association of Black Social Workers. "Our position is that the African-American family should be maintained and its integrity preserved. We see the lateral transfer of black children to white families as contradictory to our preservation efforts."[7]

However, in the book *Transracial Adoptees and Their Families,* by Rita J. Simon and Howard Altstein, the authors write:

A belief that transracial adoption is unnatural and therefore bound to be unsuccessful continues to be popular among many child-welfare professionals. Many adoption officials claim that there are studies that indicate that transracial adoption is too fragile an experience not to result in serious problems once the transracial adoptees leave their families. But to this date no data have been presented that support the belief that in the long run transracial adoption is detrimental to those involved. On the contrary, evidence accumulated by us and other researchers over more than a decade of investigating the effects of transracial adoption indicates positive results.[8]

The Child Welfare Act of 1980 says that preserving children within their own racial and ethnic heritage must be a primary concern when agencies place them with a new family. However, according to the National Center on Adoption in Washington, D.C., there are 145,000 black children who are waiting to be adopted. Is it better for them to remain in foster care than to be adopted by a white home? Most people would agree that the adoption of these children is the first priority—if there are no same-race families available, another race should be considered.

Physically Handicapped Children
In many instances, physically handicapped children are not considered hard to place. Many parents with a physical handicap are willing to adopt these children on a practical basis—their homes are already specially equipped, or they know sign language. But it is important to remember that physically handicapped children are like any others—they have the same needs, feelings, and desires. They may just require a little extra help and patience. An excellent book for parents with handicapped children is *Growing Up Handicapped*, by Evelyn West Ayrault. Born with cerebral palsy, Dr. Ayrault overcame her handicap to become a respected clinical psychologist. Her book discusses everything that a prospective parent should know about the handicapped child.[9]

Wayne and Lisa Fletcher of Dale City, Virginia, are the adoptive parents of three severely handicapped children. Wayne Fletcher himself has rheumatoid arthritis. But the Fletchers say living with the children is no problem. "We'll leave the healthy, white infants to someone who can't handle anything but a hangnail," says Lisa.

Why did they adopt these children? "There's really no explanation of why you do it. We would be old and successful now, have a nice home, if we had stayed just the two of us," says Lisa. "The kids are neat. If we could afford it and we had the space, I would like a house full. We know our limits. Three is enough."[10]

Mentally Handicapped Children

Among the hardest to place children are those who are mentally retarded. Years ago it was far easier and socially acceptable to simply place retarded children in institutions rather than find a home for them, but today mentally retarded children are available for adoption.

In the summer of 1979 I was working on a telethon to raise money for the university I attended. I happened to call a lady in Minneapolis, Minnesota who told me that she and her family of seven children would be happy to contribute.

"Seven children?" I questioned.

"Seven Down's syndrome children," she answered. "We are all one big happy family here."

Recently I called Ruth Landmark again. "Do you still have seven children?" I asked.

"Well, I only have five now," she explained. "I had my sixtieth birthday the other day and it's getting a little bit harder to keep up with everything."

We talked for a while and I learned that Ruth has been keeping Down's syndrome children in foster care for over 25 years. Over 75 children have passed through her loving home, and the people at Hennepin County Social Services have sent children of all ages. Bitsy arrived when she was only eleven weeks old and recently celebrated her nineteenth birthday in Ruth's home. "I keep them for years because these children just aren't being adopted," Ruth explains. "However, I hear that people are starting to adopt them now and that's good, because you'll never find more loving children."

Down's syndrome has degrees of severity, and some of the children are much more active than others. Many are prone to health problems, but Ruth keeps a watchful eye on them. "Some of them may not live long according to our way of thinking, but they're very happy and loving." Recent studies have shown that Down's syndrome children can progress normally, but their progress lags behind the pace of healthy children.

Other Children at Risk

Often children are labeled "hard to place" because of unknown factors. Unfortunately, many otherwise healthy infants are born in poor condition and labeled "probably retarded" due to a biological mother's alcoholism or drug use. But with love and nurturing care many of these infants can grow into lovely and healthy children. One family that we know adopted a baby boy who was the result of a late-term abortion. He survived the abortion, but doctors feared he would be little more than a vegetable. Today he is an active, intelligent seven-year-old and the apple of his parents' eyes. They stepped out in faith, trusting God to make them the parents this little baby needed, whatever his condition.

In an article in *Ladies' Home Journal,* Patricia Caporale described the first day she met the boy who was to become her son, Michael. A victim of child abuse and neglect, at three he could not talk, showed severe signs of malnourishment, and a medical examination showed signs of untreated broken bones in his legs and a possible permanent injury to his spine. "This boy has a long road to travel with no guarantees," the doctor warned Pat. "You're taking a big chance. It's quite possible there has been permanent damage to the brain."

Pat and her husband, Joe, decided to give Michael a chance. They worked with him, taught him, and loved him. As time passed, he gradually caught up with his classmates and even excelled in several areas. The Caporales plan to adopt again because "Michael brought so much joy to our lives."[11]

Other "Hard-to-Place" Considerations

Out of every 1,000 available children for adoption, three or four will never be bigger than 4'10". Little People of America (LPA), an organization that provides support for dwarfs, took an interest in these children. The adoption committees of LPA acts as a referral service for dwarf parents and social workers who know of dwarf children in need of homes. Why is it important for these children to grow up with "little" parents? According to Nancy Rockwood, a dwarf and the mother of a 10-year-old adopted daughter, "We have been down the road and we know that junior high, high school, and college are the hardest years to face when you are a dwarf. No parent can understand the difficulties unless they've been there. Our LPA parents understand."[12]

There are children who need homes who are classified as "hard to place" because they have something as simple as red hair. Others may have birthmarks, hernia, or other correctible congenital defects. Other children have problems that are not easily corrected such as epilepsy and diabetes, but these can be controlled by proper medical care. Still other children experience serious handicaps—blindness, deafness, severe limb deformities, or heart disease. These children need homes and the government has removed the financial barrier by providing subsidies for the adoption of children with medical problems.

The Rewards of Special-Needs Adoption

The Community Council of Greater New York recently published a study of special-needs adoption. A "special-needs" child was defined as one who was at least eight years old, had physical, intellectual, or emotional handicaps, or was part of a sibling group of three or more children.

The study's findings were encouraging. Ninety-seven percent of the adoptions of special-needs children were intact at the time of the study, one to four years after finalization. Seventy-five percent of the adoptive parents rated the experience as good or excellent. Only seven percent (including the three percent who experienced a disrupted adoption) found the experience less than satisfactory.

The study also found that parents reported their lives, as well as the child's, had been enhanced by the adoption. The strongest predictor of the adoption outcome was the information which had been provided to the family about the child. The more inadequate the information, the less successful the adoption.

The social worker played an important role in the adoptions studied. Workers stretched the parents' preferences regarding the special-needs characteristics the parents were willing to accept, but encouraged them to feel capable of handling the care of the special needs child.[13]

Rita Laws believes it is a tragedy to ignore the 60,000 special-needs children who wait in America for adoption. Her family has seven kids ranging in age from two to nine. Four were adopted—three through a private special-needs agency, the other through the state. She wrote in *U.S. News and World Report:*

What a joy we felt to be called with the news that we had been chosen for Antonio, a five-week-old biracial baby! When Antonio was seven and one-half months old, Joaquin was born to us. And when Joaquin was seven and one-half months old, I joked that it was time to have another baby. Little did we know that our next child had been born that week. Biracial Jessie was a state placement and a member of my American Indian tribe.

Our family is unique but not unusual. Special-needs families come in all shapes and sizes. They do not have to be married, infertile, childless, rich, homeowners, or live a 'perfect' lifestyle. Profound and positive changes have occurred in special-needs adoption in the last decade. They include subsidy programs for families already stretching a paycheck to its limit, establishment of more photo-listing books, and recruitment of minority families and single parents.

All children are lovable. If you have room in your heart, don't let anything stop you from adopting.[14]

There are blessings associated with special-needs adoption, but if you feel your family is not suitable for this type of adoption, don't feel guilty. After spending some time with a friend whose child requires constant medical attention, I realized my work could never allow me to give the same care to a similar child. You alone know what you have to offer.

Never invite a child into your home out of any reason but love and the desire to give. Perhaps after you've raised two or three children and you're more settled in your parental role you may consider one of these special children. Families who adopt these children often report that the children give much more than they take—they enrich the lives of every member of the family.

FIVE
International Adoptions

There were probably 30 other small children scampering around the orphanage yard in South Korea, but she came up to me and lifted her arms in the international gesture that says in any language, "I want a hug." I lifted her up and rocked her slowly while she hugged me. Her pretty pink dress contrasted with her dark hair and dark eyes, and I hated to put her down when it was time to leave. I put her on my lap, centered her darling face in my camera, and took her picture.

I have often thought of that little girl in the Korean orphanage. Her face smiles at me every day because I have taped that photograph over my desk. When I'm writing or typing and my mind begins to wander, my eyes inevitably fall upon her smile and I'm refreshed.

When I met her it was the summer of 1978 and I was singing with a missions team on a tour of Southeast Asia. I wasn't married and had no plans to settle down, but I kept the smiling face of that precious two-year-old girl in my heart. Four years later, when my husband and I decided to adopt, it was only natural that I should think of her and the thousands like her in foreign orphanages.

It wasn't just the relative ease of finding a child overseas that led us to an international adoption agency. The Lord led us there because He honored the desire of our hearts which was, from the beginning, a Korean baby girl. But we had studied the expense and the difficulty of international adoptions and we had instead chosen the local social service agency. But it was God's plan to bring us a child from Korea and through His plan we learned that nothing is too difficult or impossible.

With an overseas adoption, parents find themselves involved with at least two agencies. There is a United States agency which does the initial home study and paperwork and there is an agency in the foreign country which provides the children for the American agency to place. Often there is a third agency in the United States which makes children available to local agencies which have done the necessary home study reports on waiting families. In an international adoption there is a maze of paperwork: visas, passports, immigration applications, naturalization applications, and so on.

Why Consider an International Adoption?
Children from other lands are available for adoption and their needs are great. The National Committee for Adoption gives statistics which indicate that foreign placements doubled between 1982 and 1987 with 6,188 children coming from Korea and 2,060 from Latin America in 1986 alone. More than 60 percent of these children were less than one year old.[1]

When it came time for our second adoption we knew that we had found our niche in international adoption. "Why spend years waiting in the United States when there are children waiting overseas?" we reasoned. Besides, we liked the idea of having children who would relate to each other and we were already an interracial family, so what difference did one more make?

Most people think of Korea when they think of international adoptions. In Southeast Asia families are steeped in the traditions of honoring their ancestors and they are very conscious about family bloodlines. As a rule, these families will not adopt other people's biological children and as a result, poor families, unwed mothers, widows, and families with more than two children often abandon children in the hope they will find a better life.

Therefore, many Asian children have been adopted by American families. Unfortunately, political policy is now hindering the easy adoption of these lovely children. At this time, many countries are consciously trying to limit the number of children available for adoption because they do no want to be known as "orphan nations." Many countries are also trying to encourage more adoptions within their own borders.

One adoptive mother wrote *Ours* magazine and explained that once a hostile Indian gentleman in a uniform confronted her in an Indian hotel lobby. He saw this mother with her newly adopted Indian daughter and ran her through a series of intensive questions. After 45 minutes, the mother reports, "I finally convinced him that yes, I was truly going to adopt my daughter, and no, she was not going to end up in a medical experiment, as newspapers in his country had implied. I was an American, and that made him believe I had devious plans for her. Many Indian people can't imagine why we adopt one of their children or profess to love them."[2]

South America is rapidly becoming a continent of orphans. Many families abandon children simply because they cannot afford to feed them. Other children lose their parents through war or disease. Agencies which handle Latin American adoptions are springing up throughout the United States.

Considerations for International Adoptive Parents

What are the problems of international adoption? Often there are no medical or family records on the child. It is difficult to know if a child is sick or how serious are his disabilities. Usually very little is known about the physical, emotional, or social condition of his biological family. Often it is difficult to be sure the child is legally free for adoption.

These cases are rare, however, and most legitimate agencies are as thorough as possible in documenting the medical care, legal history, and personal development of the child. There have been horror stories, however, of "abandoned" children actually stolen from their mothers for overseas adoption. According to many reports, traffic in stolen children has become as lucrative as trade in narcotics, so be sure you are dealing with an established, reputable agency and not a lawyer promising you a baby for an enormous fee.

Whether adoption concerns a child from the United States or a foreign country, it is important that the adoptive parents meet all American requirements before a child is presented to them. An agency should not offer a child until all of the home study work has been completed. Prospective parents should also be sure that the fees are reasonable and legitimate— between $3,000–$6,500 is ordinary, a fee of $15,000 is not. If the fees are too high, something may be questionable about the agency's operation.

Adopting a child from another country requires special preparation. Those who seek to adopt a foreign child must be aware of the possibility that the child will be sick or handicapped. It is very likely that the child will have poor teeth, lice, or a vitamin deficiency, but don't worry—at this time, it is not likely your child will carry the AIDS virus.

In July 1987 President Reagan signed into a law a bill allowing for AIDS virus testing. Part of that law applies to the medical requirements for long-term visas, including "orphan" visas. All persons applying for any long-term visa must undergo a medical examination for signs of contagious diseases including AIDS, and all persons over the age of fifteen must undergo a mandatory AIDS virus test.

Although this law may elicit a sigh of relief from parents adopting from other countries, there are several areas of concern. First, AIDS cannot be diagnosed in a single examination. Signs of AIDS may easily be confused with signs of many other conditions such as tuberculosis and malnutrition. The tests require time, probably three or four weeks, and cost money.

The AIDS antibody may show up in an infant but be a reflection of the mother's antibody up until age fifteen months.

Dr. Jerri Ann Jenista, M.D., writes, "Just like everything else in international adoption, AIDS virus testing provides no guarantees. The statistics tell us our children are not at risk—yet. The day of high risk will come, but no one can predict when. Until then, balance your fear of the risk of AIDS abroad with common sense."[3]

Even if the child is in good health, illness will probably strike after arrival home due to the change in cultures. The child's body may be on a different time schedule, so parents should be prepared for some sleepless nights. The child will have to adjust to new food, climate, caregivers, and water! All of this takes time.

International adoption also requires a lot of paperwork. I'll never forget when Gary and I drove five hours to Washington, D.C. to apply for Taryn's visa with the Immigration and Naturalization Service. We waited in line for three hours, then were told that we had to be fingerprinted for the FBI's routine check. We rushed to a shop across the street that was just closing, managed to get our fingerprints done anyway, and then ran back to INS as they were closing the doors. We filled out the forms, submitted the fee, and swore to protect and provide for the alien for whom we were petitioning.

That was only the beginning. There were other notarized forms and statements, but we took them all in stride. Nothing was so difficult that I wouldn't do it again in a minute.

For example, the following is a list of the required documents necessary for an adoption of a child from El Salvador:

—Birth certificates of husband and wife.
—Marriage certificate.
—Financial statements for husband and wife.
—Written evidence of health drawn up by a physician.
—Home study done by an adoption agency.
—Psychological study of husband and wife.
—Written evidence of existing bank accounts.

Other international agencies may require reference letters, copies of your most recent income tax form, photographs of your home and family, and letters from the other children in the family (over age 14) consenting to the adoption. The exact requirements depend on the country of the child's origin and the United States agency's stipulations.

The International Family

International adoptions are obviously not for everyone. Adopting a child from another land immediately creates an interracial or intercultural family and many people have difficulty adjusting to the idea that their children will not resemble them. But if a family is willing to extend a hand of love across the sea, intercountry adoptions are available. The children need homes urgently, and it is likely that an adoption could be completed in a year or less, depending on your "flexibility."

For a list of agencies which handle intercountry adoptions, check the *Agency Listings* at the end of this book. I would like to emphasize the Holt agency because it is a Christian agency which places children from El Salvador, Peru, Brazil, Korea, India, Taiwan, and the Phillipines. Because Holt is largely supported by donations, they keep their fees at a minimum and place hundreds of children each year.

Check the agencies in your area first. If they are unable to place children from the country in which you are interested, they may be able to "cooperate" with another agency.

It would be impossible to compile a completed list of agencies which deal with intercountry adoption because the list changes "practically every ten minutes," according to one social worker. However, the people at International Concerns Committee for Children (ICCC) keep an up-to-date list of about 70 agencies which they will send upon request.[4]

An organization that provides excellent support for individuals interested in exploring intercountry adoption is the Organization for a United Response, commonly known as OURS. Their services include a magazine published six times a year, a telephone helpline, and information available on request. OURS also has available for sale a number of adoption and cultural materials such as ethnic cookbooks, dolls, native costumes, and storybooks.

OURS began in 1967 when ten families gathered at the Minneapolis-St. Paul airport to meet their children arriving from Korea. Today OURS has grown to include over 9,000 families and supporting professionals. The group includes families adopting children from the United States, Korea, Latin America, India, and many other countries.[5]

SIX
The Wait

Do you remember how Christmas would never come when you were a child? Did you ever lie in bed at night and wish you could sleep for three weeks so that when you opened your eyes the longed-for day would finally have arrived? I used to do that. I couldn't see the worth of all those waiting days so I vainly wished them all away.

The Lord has taught me a lot about waiting patiently and in contentment, but after two adoptions and numerous other "waiting" experiences, waiting is still difficult for me. After our first home study was completed, signed, sealed, and delivered to the state office in Virginia, I spent each day on pins and needles. Every morning when I first woke up, I would think, "This could be the day when the phone will ring and we'll be parents." At work, whenever anyone telephoned and asked for me instead of my boss, my heart stopped.

Once a month I regularly phoned my social worker and, trying hard to keep the hopeful anxiety out of my voice, would ask, "How's it going? Any news? Are you placing any babies out there?"

Helen was always encouraging, but obviously she never had any concrete news or she would have called me first. We were lucky; Helen never minded taking the time to chat to an anxious parent-to-be. I think she understood the quiet desperation of adoptive parents.

We tried to stay busy, doing things that we thought we wouldn't have the time or the money for once we had a child. I bought the set of dishes I had always wanted; we built a new bathroom in the house; and we took a nice trip to the lake. But even then it was hard to relax when we were away from our telephone, the link to our future child.

Waiting wasn't easy. Every night we prayed for the child that would be ours, asking God to bless him or her, to keep our child in safety whether born or unborn. We pleaded with God, "And Lord, please send us our child quickly."

During our time of waiting it seemed that all of our friends either delivered or conceived a baby. I know that we were in the "young couple" time of life and it was only natural that our peers would be multiplying, but I felt such mixed feelings whenever my friends announced they were pregnant. I didn't envy them the pregnancy; I was over the infertility hangup. I just envied them because they knew where their children were and when they could be expected to arrive on the scene!

I quickly discovered that most pregnant women love to sit around and compare bellies, bulges, and birthing methods. Whenever I found myself in a group of these women, I quickly wearied of the conversation and usually either left the room or pretended to be mentally engrossed in some deep spiritual contemplation. Pregnant women who knew my situation often did not know how to act around me. Some refused to discuss their coming babies, ignoring the obvious, and others exhibited an insensitivity that was hard to believe and even harder to handle graciously.

We had made no secret of our infertility or of our adoption procedure, and all of our close friends knew what we were going through. I could not believe, therefore, one friend's remark when I congratulated her on her expected fourth child. "Oh," she breezed, "well, you know, some of us have got it and some of us don't!"

One night we had dinner at a friend's house. There were

four couples present. The Coffees had their six-month-old daughter there. The McCormacks had a two-year-old, and the St. James were expecting their first child in four months. Larry St. James kept tenderly patting his wife's bulging belly and making tender pregnant jokes.

I kept my composure during the evening, but as Gary and I drove home gloom began to settle around me. I kept reminding myself of God's promises, but I felt as if I was actually fighting a vicious physical battle. I was tired of fighting to pretend it didn't hurt, fighting to be happy for other couples, fighting to keep my impatience from exploding, and fighting to speak of other trivial things but the number one thought on my mind. I fought to keep my faith, to believe in God's promise, to live each day instead of willingly casting all todays for just one tomorrow.

Every day I "survived" was like a yard gained in a battle, each week a mile and every month a major victory. I knew that months passed would never have to be regained, but I was careful to realize there was a beauty to those days without children. We had time, we had few financial responsibilities, but nothing seemed to matter as much as having someone to tuck into the empty bed in the tiny room next to ours. I used to stand in the doorway and examine the brightly colored wallpaper, wondering if it would fade before the room was ever used.

One of my best friends was given a baby shower soon after we discovered our infertility. With my pasted-on smile, I went and sat calmly through the entire event until one dear friend sympathetically patted me on the shoulder. That single gesture broke down the reserves within me and while the other guests mixed, mingled, and cooed over the cute baby outfits, I spent the rest of the evening crying in the bathroom.

From that point on, I excused myself from every baby shower and simply sent a gift along with my regrets. I was genuinely happy for my friends and their babies, but I simply couldn't put myself through nights of emotional upheaval. A friend of mine who had recently miscarried felt the same way.

"There's no sense in killing yourself," she told me. "Don't worry about what other people think. You alone know what you can and cannot do."

There were times when I felt that the home study was a joke, that we didn't have a child and we would never have a child; life had simply dealt me a hand of cards and somehow I had come up short. But whenever I was tempted to grow melancholy and blame my situation on fate, God reminded me that life is not a game of cards. It is a growing experience, and I simply had more growing to do.

One Sunday morning our pastor preached from Proverbs 13. I can't remember any of his sermon, because as he read verse 12 those words leaped through my mind and began ministering with a life of their own: "Hope deferred maketh the heart sick: but when the desire cometh, it is a tree of life."

It was my promise! Not "if" the desire cometh, but "when"! Though I know that not all proverbs are promises, but simply possibilities, the Spirit of God touched my heart and said, "This is a promise for you." Whenever the waiting got rough through the months ahead, I could smile and rejoice in the expectation of my promised tree of life!

The interminable period of waiting between the completion of the home study and the presentation of a child may seem unbearable, but there is a sort of safety in it. It's a time when you can still withdraw and keep your feelings in check. Though it may last for a few months or a few years, it is a time not of risk, but of expectation. The real difficulty begins after learning that there is a particular living, breathing child for you, yet you must wait still longer to receive him or her.

In the case of most public agency adoptions, this period between the "offering" of the child and the actual homecoming may be very short. Parents may be shown a videotape of the child on Tuesday and take him home before the weekend arrives. The same is true of an infant. In a private agency, the prospective parents are most often told of a waiting infant after the mother has signed the release forms and the interval of time when she may legally change her mind has passed. If an agency allows visitation or contact before that time, the pro-spective adoptive parents are at great emotional risk.

Friends of mine have gone through that trial. They knew of a particular baby that they could get, and even though they did not see him, they knew what he weighed, when he was born, and that he was "the most beautiful baby in the hospital." The adoptive mother counted the days and mentally computed the baby's age with each passing week. Though the family members had never even seen his face, he was deeply loved.

Gary and I invited their family over to our house on the night before their new baby was to arrive home. I knew they'd be excited and we wanted to fill the evening and give them something to do and to celebrate. During the night, my friends asked me to meet them at the adoption agency to take pictures of the time they first held their child. I was thrilled and honored to share the special moment with them, and promised them I'd be at the agency at 10 o'clock the next morning.

When I arrived promptly at 10, I was surprised to find the agency office strangely quiet. The social worker met me in the hall and abruptly told me the meeting had been canceled. If I wanted to know more, I could call my friends.

The biological mother had changed her mind. Worse yet, the young mother was using the baby as a tool against her parents: "If I can't bring this baby home, I'm not coming home," she said.

The young girl's parents countered: "If you bring the baby home, we don't want you here."

My friends were emotional wrecks. They hated to see the baby, the young mother, and the grandmother suffer. Their home, with its newly painted nursery strewn with shower gifts, felt empty. It was as though someone had died.

This particular story had a happy ending. The biological mother, though it pained her deeply to make an adoption plan for her baby, agreed adoption was in the child's best interests. The young girl returned home to resume the life of a teenager and the baby at last came home to the family who had been waiting for months. I met them at their home, this time, and finally took pictures of what truly was a blessed event.

In the case of international adoptions, like ours, it may take months for the paperwork to be processed. In late July we were told it would take four to six weeks for our child's paperwork to be done so that she could fly over; it was November before our daughter finally reached our arms.

On August 16, however, a packet of photographs from Korea reached our house. I had just finished my devotions and had prayed for some encouragement—the Lord knew I was at a low point. The postman came two hours early and the pictures were right on top of our usual junk mail.

When I first opened the pictures, all of the composite images my mind had formed shattered and suddenly I was faced with the actual image of my daughter. How adorable she was! She had lots of black hair that stood straight up like a Mohawk, a huge dimple on her left cheek, and a glorious toothless smile.

I quickly divided the pictures and sent some to the anxious waiting grandparents-to-be, and sat back and cried from sheer joy. I could not wait to have her and hold her and love her.

Then we were tested and tested again. Not long after I received those pictures, word came from our Washington agency that Taryn might not be available for adoption because of difficulties with legal papers. I sat numbly after talking to the social worker, surrounded by just-purchased Pampers. Not wanting to think about any other options, I decided to simply claim God's promise and go ahead with my preparations for her. Later, Taryn's availability was confirmed.

Only weeks away from her homecoming, however, Gary and I received a disturbing phone call. The ministry for which Gary worked was cutting positions and there was a very good chance that he would be out of a job in a matter of weeks.

I was seized by every unspeakable fear. If Gary were to lose his job, I could handle leaving our home, the city, and our friends. But I couldn't bear to lose Taryn.

Thousands of "what if's" crowded my mind. What if the agency wouldn't place with an unemployed family? What if we had to move to another state and couldn't work through the agency to which Taryn was committed? What if we couldn't get a loan to afford the adoption fee?

We fell into bed that night, utterly exhausted. My sister-in-law had send me a box of cherished baby clothes, but I didn't have the heart to go through them. Did God want us to place Taryn on the altar of sacrifice?

We had one week of uncertainty before we knew if Gary's job position would be continued. During that week, I prayed and constantly reminded myself that God had never failed me. I praised Him, knowing that unconditional praise could cost me every dream I had. I praised Him because He was giving us an opportunity to realize His great provision and loving care. I praised Him for giving me a mother's heart. I praised Him for a husband who loved me.

Through the praise, God reminded me that there were other families in our ministry who faced the same job cuts. Even if we kept our job, there would be others who would lose theirs. Through this trial I heard God's gentle reminders as He taught me: "Don't be so caught up in your private dreams that you neglect the world around you. There is more to life than this week, and more to my world than this place. What I have promised, I will perform."

He did. Within a week we were assured that Gary would not lose his job. That same week we were granted a loan for Taryn's adoption fees. In His perfect timing, the Lord had worked everything out.

Taryn's was an unusual situation because she was actually cared for in Korea by friends of mine from college days. Our second adoption, however, was more usual. After our home study was updated, we were shown a picture of Kim Sang Soo, and we knew immediately this was our Tyler. We waited for the immigration requirements to be fulfilled, and within six weeks our son was home! This process, however, can take from two months to one year, depending on the child's country of origin, how much paperwork is done in advance, the health of the child (they must be healthy to travel), and how many government snafus are avoided.

This waiting is the hardest. There is no safety zone, no place to hide your emotions, and no turning back. Now your emotions are wrapped up in a certain someone, and you have begun concrete involvement in this child's life. You have prepared a room, bought clothes and toys, and thought about a name. Your family has opened its circle, and there is a gap which will remain until your newest child arrives to fill it.

A group of papers and a small photograph represent a child who is alive and waiting somewhere to be placed into your arms. Every day that passes is hard to bear because that child may not be safe within a caring womb, but in a world that he cannot understand. Because you love the child, your natural inclination is to protect even though you are miles apart. You want to see growth and development, you want to clothe and feed the child as soon as possible, but you must let someone else do these things for a while. You must trust that the Lord will take care of your child.

Our daughter was cared for in Korea by two couples Gary and I had known while in college: the Hales and the Lugars. Susan Lugar, who acted as primary "foster mother," is the sweetest girl I have ever met. We had been high school English teachers together, and I could not have chosen anyone better to care for my baby. God knew that, and through the work and efforts of Joe and Ann and Dennis and Susan, He watched over my daughter in many marvelous ways.

But there are times when tragedy strikes during this waiting phase. Mary Ann Kuharski and her husband John had two biological and two adopted children when they heard about Vo Dinh Thanh, a Vietnamese six-or-seven-year-old who had spent his entire life in the polio wing of a Saigon hospital. The Kuharskis decided to adopt Daniel, as they called him, and sent him letters, clothing, and pictures to prepare him for his new home. They felt as if their prayers had been answered.

Several times during that spring of 1975, however, Daniel's travel plans were canceled. The Kuharskis were helpless. Finally, in April, their waiting ended. They heard that an Air Force C5-A had crashed while carrying 243 orphans out of

Vietnam. Two days later they had an official word: Daniel had been killed.

John and Mary Ann held each other and wondered if perhaps they had misunderstood the Lord's leading. How could the tragedy have been part of God's plan?

Scarcely a month later they heard of a five-year-old racially mixed Cambodian boy that needed a family. The Kuharskis knew immediately that their home was meant to be opened—again.[1]

Other families have accepted children with special medical needs only to have the children die while in hospital care. I recall that another baby accidentally suffocated on an escort flight. Tragedies do occur in adoption as they do in ordinary family life. But the God who is big enough to carry you through "ordinary" problems can also carry you through the "extraordinary" trials.

What is your child doing while you wait? If you adopt through a public agency, your child probably will have been placed in a foster home for some period of time. Children are usually kept in foster care until the biological parent's consent to the adoption is irrevocable, an amount of time that varies from state to state. If you adopt an older child, memories of both the biological and foster families may remain. You will have to deal with them. Fortunately, older children are usually not placed in the same city in which their biological parents reside.

Infants who are adopted through almost any type of agency usually spend at least one or two months in foster care. Though there are agencies which allow the prospective adoptive parents to "foster" the child until the biological mother's revocation period is up, this is unusual.

While Waiting, Keep Busy

What should you do while you wait? Is there anything that will make the waiting easier? Yes, there are things you can do, and no, nothing can really make the waiting easier. But the Christian can rest in the assurance that God has the situation under control. He knows what is best for all concerned and if He has led you to adopt, the child that is waiting for you is even now being formed and is somehow being brought to you.

Once you've been assigned a child, plunge into preparation. You and your spouse must prepare a place for him, choose announcements, childproof the house if necessary, select a doctor, call the relatives, perhaps make school arrangements, buy any special food and clothes, and more. There is much to do, but the time will pass more quickly if you're busy.

If the wait is more than a few days, try to find some project to keep yourself busy. Sew curtains or make a cradle or bed for the child's room. Start a scrapbook of all materials related to your adoption proceedings. If you are adopting an older child, you might make a book that will introduce your family. Into a photograph album or scrapbook, insert pictures of your home, family pets, you and your spouse, the family car, the grandparents, etc. You might tell the family history and begin with a wedding picture. Under each photo, write part of your story beginning with, "Once upon a time, Jim and Janet fell in love and were married."

Under a photograph of the family home, write: "A little while passed and Jim and Janet wanted to share their home with a child, so they prayed and asked God to send them a very special child. They waited and waited."

This type of introductory book would be ideal to read the first time you bring the child home. If your child is waiting overseas, you could send the book, but make sure that nothing changes after the pictures are taken. A child who is expecting two cats may be very disappointed to learn that they have disappeared. You might even take a picture of the family seated at dinner, with an empty place set for him. Show lots of food on the table and happy faces. Picture Mom and Dad smiling together.

While you are waiting, keep a diary of your thoughts. Someday your child will be thrilled to read of how earnestly you waited and prayed for his arrival. Make sure you tell of any baby showers or special visitors, and be sure to describe the day he came home in great detail. Keep a calendar of the child's first year with you regardless of his age. It is important for adopted children to feel that they have roots in your family tree, so create as many memories as you can.

If you are waiting and you feel that no one can fully understand what you're going through, call your social worker and get involved in an adoptive parents support group. They will know what you have been through, and you can talk to someone who is understanding. There are also support groups for couples struggling with infertility and families who have adopted foreign children.[2]

If your child is coming from a foreign country, try to learn as much as possible about that country. Your child may or may not be interested in racial heritage when older, but at least you will have some information to answer inquisitive questioners. You would not believe how many people seriously wondered if my Korean children would ever be able to speak English! Try cooking an ethnic dish and serve it to your family.

When the wait is nearly over, assign some major tasks for the Big Day. My last minute task was to sterilize baby bottles and arrange my kitchen cupboards to accommodate baby food and formula. It helped me to have something physical to do while I waited for the hours to pass on my daughter's homecoming day.

How long will you have to wait? I asked my social worker that question a number of times and only frustrated both of us. No one can tell you how long an adoption will take. It all depends on circumstances far beyond our control; therefore, we must depend on God. I know one couple, childless after ten years of marriage, who received an infant after only nine months of waiting. I know another couple who waited through the same agency for nearly three years before they received a child. But we all rest secure in the knowledge that God is rarely early and never late. He sends us all things in due season.

Our daughter was conceived the month after we began praying for her, so she was actively being formed and brought to us as we prayed. I know that God didn't put our daughter's biological mother in what was surely a difficult situation just so we could have a child, but I do know that God can take an unfortunate, miserable situation and make it work for good.

However long you wait, remember to treasure each day you live. You have time to mature, you and your husband have a little more time to spend with "just the two of you," you have more money, more freedom, and more time for your marriage to ripen and grow rich. God knows when the time will be right and when your child will be ready for you. Don't wish these days away while you anxiously wait—cherish them and welcome them because each new day contains a victory if you will find and declare it.

SEVEN
Facing the Public

Terms you need to know:

Real parent: any parent who is not imaginary.
Natural child: any child who is not artificial.
Your own child: any child who is not someone else's child.
Adopted child: a natural child, with a real parent who is all my own.[1]

The word is out, you are prospective adoptive parents. Your friends will begin to eye you cautiously. Casual acquaintances will take a curious interest in your sex life, and you are expected to remain unruffled if someone blurts out over coffee: "Gee, I didn't know you couldn't have kids. What's the problem?"

If you have children already, folks will shake their heads and wonder aloud if you're trying to win the Do-Gooder of the Year award. "Why in the world do they want more kids?" the ladies will ask over their coffee klatches. "They must be nuts to want to raise someone else's kids!"

No matter what your situation, your best friends may take you aside and whisper confidentially:

"What you're doing is quite admirable."

"You're just asking for trouble."

"Adoption is fine; just don't give your parents a retarded
or funny-looking grandchild."

"You should have one of your own."

"You'll regret it one day when they leave to find their real
mother."

As you pass the tedious months of waiting, pregnant wom-
en, whose bellies you have patiently watched ballooning, will
glance at you pityingly and ask, "Haven't you adopted that
baby *yet?*" As if you could go out and get one off the street
corner. Friends who don't want to hurt your feelings will ignore their children when you're around and hesitate to invite
you to baby showers.

While you are waiting, kind friends will call and ask, "How's
the adoption coming?" While you both know that it obviously
hasn't "come," it is still nice to know they acknowledge your
emotional involvement in an extraordinary process spanning
months.

When at last "the call" comes, your friends will be eager for
you and just as anxious as you are.

Our day was November 4. The day was crisp and clear even
though the leaves had been off the trees for a month. We
stepped out of our spotless house, cleaned in a frenzied burst
of energy hours before, and loaded our paraphernalia into the
car: diapers, bottle-filled cooler, camera, map, and large bag
stuffed with two rattles, three blankets, and a change of
clothes.

As we made a last-minute check of the car before our four
hour trip to the airport, Gary's best friend, Benji, pulled into
our driveway to wave us off. We drove to the airport, met our
beautiful daughter, and drove quietly home. I rode in the back
seat next to the beauty who lay sleeping in her carseat, and
tried, in semi-darkness, to read the pre-flight report prepared
by the agency just before she boarded the plane.

"She has 240cc of formula at the intervals of four hours,"

the report read. "She holds the bottle at the feeding time. She belches after formula and does not vomit." What a relief! I giggled as I read to Gary:

> "She gets peevish before sleep, so foster mother makes her sleep by carrying her on the back. She sleeps at 11 p.m. and gets up at 5-6 a.m. She moves bowels twice a day. She is fussy if her diaper gets wet.
>
> "She easily shouts if she feels good. She keeps quiet when she receives a scolding from others. She touches everything and puts it into her mouth, because she has a lot of curiosity about anything. She does not feel awkward with unfamiliar faces. She hates to be alone in a room. She tends to be mild and genial. She knows whether she is cherished."

The next few hours were a rosy storybook fairy tale. Gary and I rejoiced together as we drove the four hours back home; our new daughter blissfully slept through most of the trip. When we arrived home, we all slept well.

The next day was a circus! Friends, relatives, and neighbors dropped over to see our new arrival. For the next few months at church I could not walk from the nursery to the car without being stopped by a crowd. Fortunately, our young daughter was oblivious to the sometimes trying experience of being a celebrity.

If you adopt an older child, it might be better to shield him from the onslaught of excited friends at first. Many agencies recommend that any child be kept at home for a few weeks until they have had time to adjust to their new surroundings.

Facing Your Public

Each of you will have to learn how to face the public to a degree which depends largely on how much your child resembles you. If you adopt a child from a racial background identical to yours, you may only have to face an occasional curious inquiry from the relatives at Thanksgiving. But when my husband and I (both fair-skinned and light-haired) go out with our children, we always get a reaction of some sort.

Fortunately (and remember—I am trying to be objective), my children are irresistibly cute and always seem to win the instant admiration of strangers. But it is not easy being the mother of the cutest kids in the world.

Once when Taryn was small I spent a morning running errands. We first stopped at the building where I used to work. To run in, pick up some papers, and run back out to the car took 30 minutes because as we passed each door in the office building, someone came running out to chuck "that darling baby" on the chin or to exclaim how chubby her legs were.

Next we visited the library. I allowed Taryn to roam around in the toddlers' section as I quickly scanned a magazine article. A precocious preschooler entered the room with her mother. "Oh," she squealed, "look at that Chinese baby, Mommy!"

Groan. We next paid a quick visit to the doctor's office where I had an appointment. The nice lady doctor, whom I'd never seen before, took one look at us and said, "How cute. Are you baby-sitting?" Sigh.

We decided to try a new grocery store before we went home. At the deli counter, a fellow shopper smiled and said, "She's a real doll. Is she adopted or is she yours?"

I smiled, "She's mine and she's adopted."

The check out clerk smiled as Taryn squealed at me and she asked, "What an adorable baby. Where's your husband from?"

I grinned. "Ohio."

We've heard it all. It has been a lot of fun for Gary and me to get together and compare notes about what absolute strangers feel compelled to tell us or ask us. Some of the remarks we hear are amazing. One of the junior highers Gary worked with crinkled her nose and asked, "Well, what is Taryn going to call you? Daddy?"

A spectator at a Little League game came up to me and asked concernedly, "Are you going to tell her she's adopted?"

Watching my baby toddle by in her diapers, I answered, "Oh, it's no problem. We've already told her."

We have a favorite Mexican restaurant where we eat often. The young girl behind the counter always enjoys our international family, and one night she came over and pretended to wipe the table next to us. "I just love to watch people stare at ya'll," she grinned.

Gary and I looked at each other, expressionless; then we laughed out loud.

"Are people staring at us?" he asked. "I never realized we were such celebrities."

Another time, we were eating out when an older woman pulled up a chair to our table. "I've just got to sit here and let you tell me about these children," she said. Gary and I looked at each other in surprise as she gestured to her husband who had remained at their table. "Come on over, Harv," she called. "I told you these nice folks wouldn't mind."

There have been times when people have frustrated me. At a camp where my husband and I were volunteering, I left Taryn with a counselor who volunteered to baby-sit so I could attend a service with the campers. When I returned 30 minutes later, I could tell Taryn had been crying for me—she was going through a terrific "mama" stage and hated to be separated. The sitter, a young girl of Filipino descent, remarked, "She was crying and clinging to me so much! I think I must look like her mother." The remark stung.

Another time Taryn and I were relaxing by the side of a pool when a woman pointed to Taryn and asked a friend, "Oh, that poor baby! Do they know anything about her parents?"

"Yes!" I wanted to shout. "Her parents are right here!"

Adoptive Parents are Real Parents
Many people who do not understand adoption cannot seem to accept the fact that when you adopt a child, you are the legal, moral, spiritual, and emotional parents. There's a beautiful

poem familiar to many adoptive parents:

Not flesh of my flesh
Nor bone of my bone,
But still miraculously my own.
Never forget for a single minute,
You were not born under my heart, but in it.

—Anonymous

Rearing, disciplining, and nurturing a child in a godly home involves a lifetime of commitment. Adoptive parents earn the title of "mother" and "father."

We've also had people come up and shake our hands and say, "We think what you're doing is so admirable." If they want to think I'm a saint, that's fine, but the simple truth is that we needed our children fully as much as they needed us. We're not heroes. We don't have the means or the knowledge to rid the world of orphans and unwanted children. Our desire to have these children was not totally unselfish. Their coming filled deep needs and desires within us.

So God sent us these two and He may send us others, but we are no different than any other family. Our children arrived in a different way and we may look a little different, but we like being unique.

It is not always comfortable to be unique. Though no one has really been unkind knowingly, I have begun to wonder about the effect of strangers' frequent curiosity on my children as they grow older. Taryn, who is now four, doesn't like it. She clams up and shies away from strangers.

Handling the "Difference" of Adoption
After working with junior high school students for many years, Gary and I know that most kids go through traumas of various kinds because they feel "different." One kid may hate his freckles, another will despise being only four feet tall. If our

son or daughter feels "different" at any time in their lives, we will know that it is just a part of growing up. As with all young people, my adopted children will need to learn that God has a plan and a purpose for each of us, just the way we are. If what we look like or where we're from is unique, then we can thank God for His special touch in our lives.

I've heard that drunks and children always tell the truth, and I know that children can be among the cruelest people in the world. What will I do when other children make fun of my kids because they are adopted or Korean?

I've heard children make fun of my kids and though it makes my blood boil, I've realized that any child can be an object for derision by his peers for any reason. Perhaps it happens to all children at one time or another. Taunting is not easy for any child (or his parents) to bear. But this is a normal part of life for which all parents, adoptive or biological, must prepare their children by instilling a healthy, positive self-image.

We've tried to help our kids by explaining honestly that they are Korean, that all people are different, but that God made each of us beautiful in different ways. We teach that our family is bound together by love, not biology.

Taryn's friend Andrea is expecting a new baby in her family this summer, and at lunch the other day she asked, "Where is Andrea going to get that new baby? From her mommy's tummy or from an airplane?" For Taryn, adoption is as natural a way to add to a family as pregnancy.

When people make rather ignorant or obvious remarks about your adopted child, face them with humor. Don't be defensive or paranoid, just remember that adoption is interesting to most people and they are bound to have unfounded, vague ideas about the whole process.

Some friends of mine have adopted two Korean children, now ages seven and ten. Their seven-year-old, a boy, was shopping with his mother in a neighborhood mall when another child came up and taunted him: "Chink! Chink!"

The wise young lad of seven sternly rebuked the remark by saying, "I'm not a Chink; I'm Korean." Later though, he had to ask his mother what a "chink" was.

Adopted children of any race should be taught how to handle such situations. They must learn that most people do not understand this special way that God has of bringing families together through adoption. If you will explain it lovingly and place emphasis on how wonderful adoption is, your child can excuse the ignorance of others although it might always hurt a little.

Although even white-adopted-as-infants children may feel the sting of being "different" because of adoption, minority-race children cannot cover up their "difference." In a recent issue of *Ours,* Linda Caughey, an adoptive parent, wrote a letter to the editor about the pain minority children will inevitably face:

> No matter how much we love our kids or how pluralistic we want to think our community is, the fact is that many times throughout our lives, someone—or many some-ones—will dump on them for what they look like.
>
> Our jobs as parents isn't to hope it won't happen, but to prepare our kids for when it does happen. Just as a family would buy a handicapped-accessible home if they had a handicapped child, so should any choice of home for a family with minority-race members take into account their needs for role models, cultural awareness, and a relatively accepting environment.
>
> When our minority children are grown, people will make assumptions about them based on their race. They will be seen as different. Someday, perhaps, these differences will be universally accepted. But until that day, we walk a fine line between believing "love is enough" and understanding the reality and the pain of racism for our children.[2]

Life is a blend of joy and pain; so is the adoption experience. If you are in the adoption process and experiencing the long, tedious months of waiting, you may hear of another couple who has just received their adopted child. As tempting as it may be, don't call them and bombard them with questions about their child's adoption. While prospective parents have much in common with other couples-in-waiting, some families who adopt don't like to talk much about the adoption procedure. For reasons of privacy and because of legal concerns, they may not want to discuss the child's origin or the adoption details. Also, they may feel frustrated when talking to you because they know you're "waiting" and they can do nothing to help you. Often they just want to put the adoption procedures behind them and get on with normal family life.

One family I know had two biological children, both boys, and then adopted an infant girl. I asked them if they'd be interested in joining an adoptive parents' group. "No," said the father bluntly. "Adoption was just another way to add to our family. I don't enjoy talking about my two experiences in the labor room, and I'm not going to dwell on the adoption experience, either."

Motives Make a Difference

I learned that people have different motives for adopting. There are "traditional" adopters, who choose a normal route of adoption where babies and parents are matched. Few couples today have the luxury of being traditional adopters.

On the other hand, there are "preferential" adopters who choose to expand their families (which may already include biological children) regardless of how the children are perceived by society.

Patricia Irwin Johnson writes: "Because society is not supportive of adoption, most adoption-built families of the past coped with their role handicap by rejecting its differences, preferring to try to ignore the adoptive status and to 'blend in' so that their families would be seen as 'real.' "[3]

However, according to H. David Kirk, a Canadian sociologist:

The most successful adoption-built families are those who are able to consistently acknowledge differences, since, in doing so, and in acknowledging that adoption brings both gains and losses to adoptive parents and children, these families will establish a greater empathy and understanding for one another that will build successful channels for ongoing communication.[4]

Few families today try to "hush up" their adoptive experiences, but there are many who don't enjoy the constant reminder that their children are somehow "different." If you are beginning the adoption paperwork, you will be eager, hopeful, and desperate; the family who is completing an adoption will be tired, thankful, and protective of their family's privacy. Of course there are some families who would love to talk to you and will have no qualms about telling you every detail of their adoptions. Fine. But let them take the initiative.

After a child has been placed in your family, you will be approached by people who also want to adopt. I was sought after by many people who were interested in adoption. Many nights my phone rings and a desperate man or woman will ask, "I've heard that you've adopted children. Could you give me some information?"

I have always tried to help couples who could not have biological children, but I must admit that I have been irked by people who want a foreign child because "they are so cute." After I mention the difficulties and expense, most of these families are easily dissuaded. Adoption is not for people who give up easily.

The Extended Family
Adoption is for families—and we mustn't forget the extended family. Your child must not only be integrated into your immediate household, but also must become a part of the family that meets at Aunt Irene's every Thanksgiving: grandparents,

aunts, uncles, cousins, in-laws, and miscellaneous relatives.

Our children have been welcomed into my extended family with open arms. Their cousins enjoy having such unique relatives. Eight-year-old cousin Shane once featured baby Taryn's photographs in his school's "Show and Tell." The aunts and uncles are supportive and our parents love our kids as much as they love their biological grandchildren.

During your home study your social worker will invariably ask how your parents will feel about an adopted child. You'll only know if you talk to your parents about adoption before you begin your plans. They may need some time to adjust to the idea.

Our infertility was probably as big a hurdle to my parents as it was to us. At first it was a shock, a disappointment, and an occasion for grief to them as well. My mother was eager to see the qualities she admires in me reproduced in her grandchild. In her eyes, the major problem with adoption was that it would not be a biological reproduction of Angie running around the house. Actually it is a sort of family pride: my grandmother was a singer, my mother is a singer, I am a singer—what? no daughter to be a singer? I don't think the disrupted legacy bothered me half as much as it bothered my mother.

But God has a way of comforting and changing hearts. Through the months that we waited for Taryn and as we began to see the Lord's hand in bringing her to us, my mother was convinced. God had obviously intended this little girl for us. Such a special child would have distinct abilities and qualities all her own. She would be blessed by entering a Christian family and she would bless us simply by being herself.

How could we argue with the goodness of God? We can't. And we won't. We are simply thankful beyond belief that God has done such a marvelous thing for us. For months after my children arrived home, whenever I was invited to sing and share with a Sunday School class or another group meeting, I dissolved into tears if I spoke of my children. Even now I tiptoe into their rooms, watch them sleeping, and rejoice to think how God has blessed us. Every child, no matter what his or her heritage, abilities, or talents, is a gift from God.

In time, you can learn to face the public with aplomb. There is a young Oriental man in our doctor's office who always begins to jabber in an unknown (to me) tongue to my kids, but I can cope with him. Unthinking people will always express amazement that my children speak English, but I can cope with them too. Mannerly people who would never dream of approaching a stranger and asking, "How did you get to be so fat?" will approach me and ask, "Where on earth did you get that Chinese child?" I can even cope with them. Experience has made me mellow.

Charlton Heston, one of my favorite actors on screen and off, has learned to handle questions. He has two daughters, one biological and one adopted. When asked which is which, Heston always replies, "I forget."

EIGHT
Your New Child Is Home

Meeting Taryn and Tyler at the airport was almost anticlimactic—each time, we simply packed them up, changed their diapers and their clothes, and walked out the door. We didn't have to sign any papers or take any vows—we simply took them home. Both "labors" were difficult, but the delivery was relatively painless.

The adjustments were something else. Taryn became sick the day after her homecoming and because I was a new mother, her simple cold and diarrhea scared me to death. I frantically called our family doctor less than 24 hours after her arrival.

Her first few hours home were beautiful. She greeted each visitor with smiles and playful cooing before breaking out in a fever that evening. Not only did she become ill, but Gary and I did too. We three were up and down at all hours of the night and none of us had the energy to do anything but drag ourselves around the house. I remember hanging over her bed at two o'clock in the morning, nauseated but trying to stay on my feet until she went to sleep. She cried and I lifted her up only to feel vomit dripping down my back and my nightgown clinging to me in smelly stickiness.

For a few hours I actually dreaded the sight and smell of the baby's room and wondered aloud if I was cut out for this mothering business. "Please, God," I begged, "it has to be better than this."

But all the misery quickly passed and in a week I became "super mother." I knew all about Pedialyte and vaporizers, and found myself conversing with other mothers about the advantages of tepid baths for fever as if I had been doing it all my life.

If you are planning to adopt an infant but unsure of how to care for a baby, find your nearest hospital's obstetrical department and inquire about classes in baby care. Also, you might buy one of the many good books on infant care.[1]

For information on breastfeeding your adopted infant, contact your local La Leche League. Breastfeeding is possible, and those who have done it say there is nothing like the experience.

The rough period of adjustment is different with each child. Taryn had arrived in our home on November 4, 1983 and I believe she was well-adjusted within one week. On April 13, 1985 we received Tyler from the same airport. His adjustment period lasted at least two months.

On that April night I could not help but remember the other time we had stood in the same terminal—then we were anxious and naive, now we proudly kept an eye on our scampering two-year-old as we waited with the usual assortment of bottles and diapers, along with four other sets of parents.

When the plane finally arrived two hours behind schedule, we mothers were allowed to go on the plane and pick up our children. The ladies formed a line and scanned the passengers who were disembarking, not looking at their faces, but for the end of their line. When only the babies and their escorts remained on the plane, we hurried down the ramp and into the airplane cabin.

Tyler was the first baby I met. He was small, barely fourteen pounds at seven months of age. I took him from the social worker and gave him a quiet welcome kiss. I could have walked off the plane right then, but I stopped to watch the tender scene around me. The gentle mothers and beautiful babies greeted each other in a touching tableau and I wanted to stand still and imprint the memory in my mind.

The flight crew, tired and impatient, reminded us they needed us to leave so they could clean the plane, so we broke the spell of that first welcome and rejoined our families in the terminal. Taryn was excited about her new baby brother. Gary was thrilled but a little awkward with this tiny one. Like the other mothers, I put him down to change his clothes and instantly I was alarmed. Tyler couldn't sit up. As I changed him and spoke soothingly to him, I had a strange feeling we were headed for a difficult adjustment.

I was right. Tyler the Terrific (who is alternately Tyler the Terror) has been through a lot. His first week with us was pure honeymoon. He was easy to put to bed, healthy, and blissfully pleasant. He adapted easily to his strange bed, new food, and foreign faces.

Then he began to protest with a vengeance. He became sick and after an examination by our family doctor, I was told Tyler was undersized, undernourished, and developmentally delayed. There was nothing we could do but be strong and work it out.

At eight months old, Tyler couldn't hold a bottle, sit up, or crawl. He didn't babble, put any weight on his legs, or eat solid food. After one month of my intensive "feed and fatten" program, he still only weighed in at the fifth percentile on the doctor's weight chart. It was obvious Tyler was going to need time and attention and an aggressive exercise program.

Our social worker called to see how things were going and I told her about Tyler's difficulties. "So you are concerned?" she asked.

"Yes, I'm concerned," I replied, "but I certainly am not saying I want to send him back."

As I worked with him, desperately wanting to feel that this baby and I shared a mutual love, he refused to meet my eyes. When I carried him he would lay his head against my chest as if he were too timid to lift it up to explore. He was sweet-natured and snugly, but I knew this behavior was not typical of a curious eight-month-old.

After talking and rocking and singing to him for hours, I would fall in bed and confess, "Gary, it just feels like he is not really my baby. It's like I'm taking care of him for someone."

As I gently held him and fed him his bottle, he would look into my eyes for a second and then stare over my shoulder. I later learned this is typical behavior for babies who have been hospitalized for long periods of time—they learn to not emotionally attach themselves to one person for fear that person will eventually leave.

Tyler wanted to be held constantly. He screamed violently when I placed him on the floor to play. He had no nap schedule and could not understand when I placed him in his bed after lunch. For two weeks I sat in the hall and listened to him cry. I knew it would take time for him to learn that we had not deserted him, but his screams broke my heart.

We entered him into a physical therapy program offered by our city's health department and for hours we taught him how to stack blocks, pick up toys, and concentrate on one task. Every day I would place Tyler in a crawling position, place a folded dishtowel around his chest, and walk on my knees lifting him by the dishtowel just enough so that he could "crawl" as I walked.

All the work eventually began to pay off. At 10 months he began to crawl. He babbled, "Ba, ba, ba" constantly when he was exploring and there was no sweeter sound to my ears. He sat fascinated for hours and watched his big sister play. He ate well, learned to sleep on a schedule, and was curious and eager to explore. Most important, he learned to love us. Gone forever were his averted eyes and emotional distance. Though it took some time, Tyler had at last bonded to us.

Why was Tyler delayed? I can only guess. Perhaps he was moved from one foster home to another. It is likely that he was carried much of the time in the Korean way on his foster mother's back—that would explain why he liked to be held and his tendency to take cat naps instead of a scheduled nap. We did learn that he had been hospitalized for an entire month when he was two months old.

But none of that really matters now. Tyler is here, he is a bundle of energy and we love him totally.

The Stages of Adjustment

Each child's adjustment is different, but most pass through some of the same stages. All children, even infants, experience grief when they are separated from their foster parents. Adopted children have experienced rejection and insecurity, and one of the major jobs of the adoptive parents is to instill trust and a sense of belonging.

Although infants experience a stage of grief, they usually are able to pass through it quickly. Social workers believe that this stage may be particularly difficult for infants because they lack the verbal skills necessary to express their sense of loss.

Older children experience a more involved adjustment experience. The first stage is known as the *honeymoon* period because, at that point, everything is blissful. Children may act happy and behave perfectly, although they may manifest an illness or a change in appetite. When children do this, they are actually experiencing shock over the loss of the foster home. It is difficult to believe in the loss of all familiar things and people, and just as difficult to believe this new relationship will last.

The next stage is the *protest* period. Children begin to realize that there will be no returning to the former home, and the perfect angel disappears. Children may be disobedient, cry for no reason, or withdraw into a sulky silence. This stage may last for several months, and the parents may be convinced that they have brought a "holy terror" into their home. Parents should not ask "why" the child is behaving in a certain way because he probably will not be able to tell you. Parents might find it helpful to let the child know that he or she is understood by making statements like, "Lots of kids think their new home will not be as happy as their last home. That fear usually goes away," or "If I was lonely for my foster mother, I'd feel angry at my new mother too. It is okay to feel angry, but I hope you will tell me about it the next time you do."

Eventually children will realize that there is no going "back home" to the foster parents, and will enter the stage of *despair*. During this stage children will often take on a hopeless character. They will withdraw into gloomy solitude and prefer to be left alone. They still do not trust the new home, and will react excessively to small hurts and disappointments. Despite their children's attitudes, it is important that the parents continue to reassure them by displaying their physical presence and loving support.

Finally, children will reach the stage of *acceptance*. During this stage they finally are able to separate themselves from the past. They will then be able to reach out and form new relationships. They may still think about the past, but it will not be the basis for future emotional involvements. Realizing the future can bring happiness to them, they will gradually begin to live in the promise of the present.

Although the variations of this process will vary from child to child, parents should be aware of what is happening in the child's mind. Children who are actively grieving may have trouble concentrating or following directions. Hence, a school-age child may have trouble. One may appear aloof, forget to do one's homework, bother the other children, and seem easily distracted. A grieving child may even be diagnosed as having a learning disability when it is simply a matter of trying to adjust to a new life. Don't panic; simply give your child time to adjust.

Parents may wish to consider keeping older children out of school for a month or so to help with the adjustment problems. Other parents feel that their newly adopted children should be immediately involved in a normal routine, but it may be more important to give your child some time to cope with such a major upheaval.

Your Child's Personal Past

No matter what the age, your adopted child has a past history of which you are not a part. Parents should resist the impulse to try to cover up the past. Do discuss the adoption process, but emphasize the new family relationships.

Candace Wheeler, a social worker who has written an excellent book titled *Moving In: Adopting Older Children,* offers the following advice:

> If your child has a scrapbook or photo album about his past, keep it available on a shelf for him to look at whenever he wants; hiding it won't "keep his mind off it." Keep making affection available to him; reach out to him. Don't wait for him to "ask for it." And don't give up. When the going is roughest is when he needs you most to see him through.[2]

It is very important for parents to understand why their children are not with their biological parents. With the rare exception of orphans and some international adoptions, children are separated from their parents because of voluntary relinquishment or the judicial termination of parental rights.

Parents who voluntarily relinquish their children realize that they do not have the skills or means (or both) necessary for the task. Those who are separated from their children by the court demonstrate their inability to be proper parents. It is important to remember that these biological parents were not evil; they were simply not competent.

What do you tell your child? Something must be said because all children think about their roots—it's a part of their identity. If you decide to discuss the "bio" parents only when you are asked about them, you may be waiting forever. Children know if you're comfortable with a subject, and if you'll approach the topic confidently, your child will be put at ease.

Your child will need to know the simple truth—that the biological parents were not able to give proper care. You don't have to explore the painful details. Also, avoid picturing the birth mother as a martyr who loved the child so deeply that she released him for adoption. Although many young women make adoption plans out of an unselfish love, the reasons of others revolve around personal convenience. Don't paint a rosy romantic picture; be as realistic as possible.

The most important aspect of a child-parent relationship is honesty. If your child asks you about the biological parents, you must be prepared to tell what you know appropriate to the child's level of understanding. If you know nothing, say so.

You may feel threatened by your child's request for information about "other" parents, but psychologists assure us the chances of a child leaving are extremely slim. Adoptive parents are the true psychological parents. And as supportive, honest parents, you must be prepared to help your child's search for roots.

The prospect of your child leaving to search for her "other mother" may make your blood run cold, but if your child expresses such an interest, be supportive. Any active search for biological parents should not take place until your child has passed through the tumultuous teenage years and into adulthood. Your child should also be advised of the possible need and right of the biological parents to maintain confidentiality.

Alfred A. Messer, an Atlanta psychiatrist, suggests that at the time of placement, the biological mother and the adoptive parents write letters. Many adoption agencies have begun this practice.

The first letter, from the biological mother, should be addressed to the child. In the letter she should explain why she made an adoption plan for the child, conveying reassurance that her choice was "difficult and made only out of love and concern, not malice or whim." This letter should be given to the social worker, who will in turn, give it to the adoptive parents to be held for the child.

The second letter should be written by the adoptive parents to the biological mother. They should express their deepest thanks for the child, give the child's first name, and tell something about their home. Dr. Messer suggests that the couple "mention their struggle to have a child and let the mother know how happy they are." They should also promise to share the biological mother's letter with the child when they feel it is proper.

Dr. Messer believes "by removing some of the child's uncertainty about his origins, a letter from his birth mother helps diminish his feelings of rejection and abandonment and provides the basis for a healthier self-esteem."[3]

When to Tell Your Child About the Adoption

When should you tell your child that he or she is adopted? Most experts advise telling your children of their adoption before they are able to understand. A child should not learn of the adoption through a sudden revelation or a shocking confession.

Perhaps the best time to explain adoption is at age three or four when your child begins asking the first questions about "where do babies come from?" Children of this age are able to understand that pregnant women have babies in their tummies, and they can also understand that some babies come into families through adoption. You don't have to detail the circumstances of the biological parents, just say, "God brought you into our home by adoption."

When your child is old enough to want more specific answers, you can explain that not all women who carry babies are able to take care of them. "But God watches over those babies," you can explain, "and He brought you to our home where there is lots of love to share." Meeting other adopted children will help your child understand that adoption is a common, natural process.

Ellen Clore, director of the nurse practitioner program at the University of Virginia, advises that children should hear the word "adoption" long before they are capable of understanding it. She also stresses, "Before the age of five, address the issue, because a child needs to hear it from parents—not teachers or friends. Trust must be preserved." Clore adds that research has proven "it's not always what parents say that's most important in the early years, but rather the emotional environment and tone in which they say it."[4]

We have integrated adoption into our conversation quite naturally. When she was only 18 months old, one of Taryn's favorite books was titled *The Chosen Baby*. It's a delightful story for preschoolers about an adopted baby. Through this story children learn that adoption is natural, that it happens to other people, and that adoptive parents love their children very much.[5]

Children and Their Adoptions

How do adopted children feel about their adoptions? According to Laurie Flynn, former director of the North American Council on Adoptable Children, most children go through a stage where they say they hate their parents and would like to run away. "It's very upsetting," says Flynn, "but parents must not overreact. Instead, get at what's making the child fearful. Usually the child wants reassurance. The parents can say, 'You are my child. I am your parent. Let's work this out.' "[6]

Steve and Debi Standiford decided to adopt two adolescent Vietnamese boys. The adoption progressed well at first; then Nhi, whose legs were useless because of polio, realized that no American doctor was going to be able to fix his legs so he could run like other boys. He had to learn to walk using crutches, and he was bewildered when Steve and Debi insisted that he become independent.

To Nhi, who remembered that handicapped persons in Vietnam were tended totally by family members, his parents' unwillingness to wait on him was a sign they didn't care. One day when he was home alone, Nhi swallowed drain cleaner. Fortunately, his brother arrived home in time to call an ambulance.

The Standifords thought the adoption had failed miserably, but through that difficult experience the family learned to communicate. Nhi and his brother explained that a cultural difference had caused Nhi's misunderstanding, and together they were able to work through the traumatic experience.[7]

Of course, no one person can describe all the feelings of all adopted children, but the following is a letter from an adult adoptee. The trials and upheavals of her teenage years are past, and this adult offers a beautiful perspective on adoption:

> I feel special because I am adopted. My birthparents loved me enough to give me life and to make a good plan for me. My adoptive parents loved me enough to call and wait; to interview and wait; to plan and wait; and wait and wait and wait for me.
>
> I'm thirty now, but I've known I was adopted for as long as I can remember. The account of all the special arrangements made for me was one of my favorite bedtime stories as I grew up.
>
> I always loved to hear about the phone call from Hope Cottage which my parents received: "You can come pick her up this afternoon." About the pink dress that I wore, and how all the relatives and neighbors rushed over to greet me at my new home; and how the judge told my parents, "She's yours now. You can't give her back! Let me see her picture!"
>
> And later, about how my prayers for a brother were answered when we adopted him. I have always felt secure in this; I knew I was wanted and planned for.
>
> My husband and I have two adopted children of our own now. What a joy they are to us! We love to tell them their own special bedtime stories.[8]

When telling your children about their adoptions, avoid candied phrases such as "we chose you above all the others," because they are inaccurate. Don't bring home a pet and explain that you are adopting him in the same way as your child—too many pets meet unfortunate ends or are given away. Your child doesn't need that kind of insecurity.

Candace Wheeler suggests:

One of the best ways to help a child gain an understanding of his past experiences and of the ways he came to be with you is through a "story." Written in language appropriate to the child's age, often with his help, it is his very own story, beginning at his beginning and bringing in his foster placement, foster care moves, the reason for adoptive placement, and the story of his coming to you. Perhaps your caseworker can construct a story for your child, or help you write your own.[9]

Inner Family Relationships

How do you prepare biological children for the arrival of an adopted child? In the same way you would prepare them for another biological child. As soon as you begin the adoption proceedings, bring talk of "your new brother" or "your sister" into family conversation. Let your children take an active part in preparation for the new child and upon arrival safeguard the family's privacy so that the children can admire the new one without competing with strangers.

Remind your "bio" children that the adopted child is just as much a part of the family as anyone else. I am acquainted with one family with two "bio" girls and an adopted infant boy. The youngest daughter immediately fell in love with "mothering" the new addition, but the oldest girl deliberately distanced herself. One afternoon I asked her, "How's the new baby?"

She flatly replied, "He doesn't feel like my brother yet."

Like adults, children need to be reminded that much of life is based on fact, not feelings. This older girl eventually, through time and direct involvement, realized that her family was no longer complete unless the adopted son was present.

Many adoptive parents face doubts about their own abilities. "Will he love me as much as he would love his foster or biological parents?" they may wonder. The answer is not in the child—it is in the parent. Adoptive parents are easily able to love an adopted child as much as a biological child, so why should they wonder about their children's ability to love? If a child is given the freedom to love the others who have been in his life, his love will be returned. Love is not exclusive; we can love as many people as we know. The more we love, the greater our capacity to love.

Christ said, "My command is this: love each other as I have loved you" (John 15:12, NIV). Because He loved us, we have the ability to love. Likewise, if your child is given the freedom to love both the foster and biological parents she may remember, you can know that she will be able to love you.

Once home your child is to be treated as you would any child. An old acquaintance came to visit us not long ago and he and his new wife were quite taken with our kids' baby pictures. "You see, Angie," the man explained, "we want to have one of *our own*"—I winced—"and then adopt one. So tell me how raising a Korean child is different from raising a normal child."

As graciously as I could, I explained that my children were my own, and though sometimes people noticed our "interracial-ness," I had the same concerns with raising my kids as any parent. Adopted children still have to be potty trained, fed, disciplined, educated, and loved.

After Taryn had been home for about a month, we decided it was time to establish a bedtime and stick to it. Her foster parents had walked her to sleep, but that wouldn't work for us. She had grown so heavy that my back ached from carrying her and she always woke up when I put her in the bed anyway.

In one of those indispensable books about baby care, I read that few children like to go to bed. Amen. But the security of a designated bedtime is important, and we wanted to establish a secure routine for Taryn as soon as possible. We decided on the "bedtime routine." We went in together, diapered and dressed her and said a prayer. Sitting together on the floor, we read Margaret Brown's charming book *Good Night, Moon*, finishing, we walked around the room and said goodnight to each object: "Goodnight, clock. Goodnight, bear." Then we gave Taryn a hug and kiss and put her in the bed . . . and held our breath.

On the first night she screamed for 40 minutes. Every 10 minutes we went in to reassure her and wipe her nose, but we didn't pick her up. Finally she slept and we breathed easier.

On the second night, she screamed for 20 minutes. We sat in our room, horrified by her screams and bothered by doubts and insecurity. Were we doing the right thing? But she finally slept.

On the third night, she screamed loudly—once. That was all. She had learned. Bedtime became natural, normal, and nicely final.

I told the story of our "bedtime experiment" to some friends. One lady remarked, "I don't know how you could just sit there and let that child scream. Think of all she's been through!"

Adoptive parents, like all parents, need to extend firm security, not wavering pity. As with all discipline, rules and boundaries are an expression of love and concern. Don't be so caught up in pity that you cannot be firm when your child needs someone to count on.

Love in Words and Actions

How can you assure your child that he or she is loved? The following points, according to psychologist Clyde Narramore, will help you to assure your adopted children that they are loved and treasured.

Although psychologists tell us that all children have several basic needs, one of the greatest of these is *love*. One of the easiest ways to express love is simply to *say it aloud*. Say it several times a day—at bedtime, in the morning, when coming in or going out. How can your children learn to express or give love unless they know they are loved? Those three little words, "I love you," will never grow trite or worn out through use, but only more precious.

I grew up in a family which, though wonderful in many ways, did not often verbally express love. Fortunately for my children, my husband grew up in a demonstrative family and it has been easy for me to learn to tell my children how much I love them. Recently Taryn was engrossed in coloring a picture, but she stopped long enough to look up at me and say, "I love Daddy." I smiled and answered, "I love him too." Those are wonderful words.

Another way we show a child love and respect is by *not yelling*. Most of us would never yell at our friends, no matter how annoyed or angry we were. Why is it so easy to yell at our children? Anger does not accomplish anything. A firm voice, backed up by the proper discipline, will show children you love and respect them enough to treat them fairly.

By *spending time* with a child you may also demonstrate security and love. Dr. Narramore shared with me the following story: "I was giving an IQ test to a little boy one time when he looked up and said, 'You know something, Mister?' "

" 'What?' I asked."

" 'My daddy loves me.' "

"I said, 'Your daddy loves you? But how can you be sure?' "

"He said, 'Because he likes to play with me.' "

"Now that was pretty simple," smiled Dr. Narramore, "but that's very deep. We know people love us when they spend time with us."[10]

A fourth way to tell children you love them is to *encourage them to do the talking*. As an adult, you choose friends who will let you talk and with whom you feel comfortable. If you love your child, you'll encourage talking about anything and everything.

What if your child wants to talk about the adoption? Let this occur. When Taryn was three, she would often climb into my lap and beg, "Tell me the story about when I came over in the airplane and Daddy held me and Mommy gave me a ba-ba, and you took me home." A child, sensing your unwillingness to discuss a subject, will hesitate to mention it, but the forbidden topic will fester in the imagination.

All aspects of your adoption experience do not have to be public knowledge, but your child should feel free to discuss anything about the adoption—just be sure your discussion remains appropriate for the child's age-level.

Encourage and compliment your child. Even when a childish effort is far from adult perfection, find something good in the effort and praise it: "Your piano playing sounds so good. Doesn't it make a pretty sound?"

To assure that your child is loved as an individual, *never compare him with a brother or sister.* Your child is his own person. A child held up to unfavorable comparisons will hate the one who does the comparing, the one he's compared to, and himself because he can't seem to measure up.

Another way you can tell a child you love him is to *lead him in paths of righteousness.* We give our most precious gifts to those we love the most, and the knowledge that God is in the world and the Creator of it is the greatest gift of all.

Teach the Bible and its principles to your child as early as possible. Take a walk with your child and point out the trees that God made and the birds who follow His seasonal direction. God designed everything; let your child see and learn about life.

Dr. Narramore suggested that parents lead their children to the Lord at an early age. "Really it doesn't take an awful lot of mature intelligence to realize that you've done things that are wrong, that sin displeases God, and that God sent Jesus Christ to die for us. Children can use computers at three and do all kinds of mathematical equations by the time they're four. As they keep getting older, just explain more of the Gospel at their age level."

"I think it may be detrimental to a person's intellect to live in this world without understanding that God made it. It is going through life without the facts," Dr. Narramore believes.[11]

No matter what your child's heritage, age, color, or background, love is your best tool. Teach in words and lead in actions to Jesus Christ and God will bless your adoption plan.

After the Placement

After your child is home, your social worker is required to make post-placement visits. Helen visited us three times, one visit every two months. I didn't really know what to expect, but, knowing Helen, I figured that the visits would be more like friendly gatherings than formal interrogations.

I was right. During each visit, Helen and I would sit and watch Taryn or Tyler play. I'd tell her about their latest escapades and she'd talk about the latest adoption placements through the agency. I'll admit that I was a little cautious, but I even dared to tell her about Taryn's eating a piece of wrapping paper and nearly choking. I knew she wouldn't think I was an incompetent mother just because we had typical baby incidents.

You should always be honest. The social worker will not be shocked to learn that you sometimes feel like walking out of the house and moving (alone!) to another state. These feelings are normal and are to be expected during the difficult times of adjustment.

Unfortunately, though, some adoptions do not work. In these cases, the social worker usually learns of the difficulty through the home visits or through a frantic parent's phone call. But these cases are the exception rather than the rule. If an adoption is disrupted, the child will be removed from the home and placed in foster care until another adoptive family can be found.

One family I know was waiting for a preschooler from Korea. They were told they might have a long wait because babies were plentiful and preschoolers scarce. But there was good news! An adoption had disrupted, and a lovely four-year-old Korean girl needed a home "ASAP." This family adopted her, had a smooth and beautiful adjustment into their already large family, and even managed to save on air-fare fees!

When the post-placement visits are done and the trial period required by the state has passed, a lawyer provided by the agency or engaged by the adoptive parents will file the adoption in court. Copies of the petition, original birth certificate, home study report, post-placement report, and other papers are passed among the various state agencies until everything has been investigated and approved.

Taryn had been home for nearly a year when I found the official-looking envelope in the morning mail. When I opened it, I read that the circuit court had "adjudged, ordered, and decreed" that our daughter was "entitled to all the rights and privileges, and subject to all the obligations, of a child of said Petitioners born in lawful wedlock." I telephoned my husband who was at work: "Honey! We're legal!"

NINE
How Does God View Adoption?

As you pursue adoption, you will doubtless consider how your family, your friends, and perhaps your own children feel about the procedure. Have you stopped to consider how God feels about adoption? Most Christian adoptive parents will diligently pray for wisdom as they decide to adopt and select an agency, but it is also wise to study the Scriptures to understand the special bond God honors through adoption.

Adoption—the legal act of investing with sonship—occurred often in the Old Testament. Abraham adopted Eliezer before Isaac was born and declared him his heir, Joseph's sons were adopted under Jacob, Moses was adopted by Pharaoh's daughter, and Mordecai adopted his niece, Esther. And in another sense, Samuel was "adopted" by the priest Eli after Hannah placed him in the Lord's service. Even Jesus was adopted by Joseph the carpenter, His earthly, but not biological, father.

The nation of Israel was spiritually adopted by God and subsequently blessed. The Lord told Moses, "Thus saith the Lord, Israel is My son, even My first-born" (Ex. 4:22). Paul wrote of his fellow Jews: "The people of Israel, theirs is the adoption as sons; theirs the divine glory, the covenants, the receiving of the law, the temple worship and the promises" (Rom. 9:4, NIV).

Later the Gentiles were spiritually adopted by God and we as Christians are now the sons of God. In his letter to the Gentiles in Rome, Paul encouraged them: "For ye have not received the spirit of bondage again to fear; but ye have received the Spirit of adoption, whereby we cry, Abba, Father. The Spirit itself beareth witness with our spirit, that we are the children of God" (Rom. 8:15-16).

Because we have been adopted, God has blessed us with a new nature and name, fatherly love and discipline, access to Himself, and a marvelous inheritance. Having set such an example, isn't it reassuring to know that we can follow that model in our earthly families? Just as the union between Christ and His church can be a symbol of Christian marriage, so our adoption by the Heavenly Father can represent the bond between adopted children and their families.

Salvation: A Beautiful Picture of Adoption

Dr. Harold Willmington writes of how the word "adoption" fits into the vocabulary of salvation in his *Willmington's Guide to the Bible,* from which I have drawn the following information.

The word "adoption" literally means "the placing of a son." Adoption logically follows regeneration. Regeneration gives one his nature as a child of God, whereas adoption gives him his position as a son of God.

Spiritual adoption differs from civil adoption in several ways. First, we never adopt our own biological children, but God never adopts any other than His spiritual children. Civil adoption provides a comfort for the childless, but God already had a beloved Son prior to adopting us. There are usually many pleasing characteristics in a civilly adopted child, but not in God's children prior to their adoption (Rom. 3:10-18). Civil adoption could never give the child the nature of the father, but God's adopted are given the very mind of Christ (1 Cor. 2:16). In some cases, civil adoption could be declared null and void, but God's adopted are absolutely secure.

Spiritual adoption is similar to civil adoption in other ways: first, the Father (parent) must begin the action leading to adoption (Isa. 1:18; John 3:16). Both types of adoption give an inheritance to one who previously had none (Rom. 8:17; 1 Peter 1:1-9). Lastly, both types of adoption provide a new name (John 1:42; Rev. 2:17) and a new home.[1]

When your adopted child is old enough to understand the plan of salvation, he can better understand his position as an adopted child in your family and in the family of God if you will use the Scriptures to explain the matter to him. It is the will of God that we all be spiritually adopted, and it will be a comfort to your child to know that it was the will of God that brought him to you, as well.

Children with a Difficult Past

If your child comes from a difficult background, let him know that his life is a special gift from a loving and concerned God. Despite what your child knows or does not know about his biological roots, you can teach him that God is a "father of the fatherless" (Ps. 68:5) and He has a plan for each of us. " 'For I know the plans I have for you,' declares the Lord, 'plans to prosper you and not to harm you, plans to give you hope and a future. You will seek Me and find Me when you seek Me with all your heart' " (Jer. 29:11, 13, NIV). These promises can bring great comfort.

When they are mature enough to understand, you can help children who were abused, illegitimate, or abandoned accept themselves and their pasts by explaining that while they may be affected by the problems of their biological parents (particularly children who are older when adopted), God does not and will not hold them accountable for any sins committed by the birth parents.

Is this an issue which you must consider before adopting? Yes. In your home study you may be asked if you are willing to accept a child whose biological mother is a drug addict . . . or a prostitute . . . or serving a prison sentence. Perhaps one of the biological parents committed suicide. These problems do not have to affect your adopted child beyond his or her adoption placement, but they may affect you if you haven't seriously considered the issues.

Ezekiel 18:20 (NIV) reads: "The son will not share the guilt of the father, nor will the father share the guilt of the son. The righteousness of the righteous man will be credited to him, and the wickedness of the wicked will be charged against him." The truth of this Old Testament passage vindicates the adopted child from any prior familial trespasses. The child is like any other human being, individually responsible to the Lord for his or her actions.

It is true that many adopted children would not have been placed for adoption except for the sins or problems of their biological parents, but if you, as adoptive parents, build moral and spiritual character into your children, they can overcome inherited character faults or flaws. Nurturing such growth is one of the great joys of adoptive parenting.

Many people believe that character deficiencies, like physical disorders, may be passed on from parent to biological child. For instance, if one parent has a severe temper problem, the child may exhibit the same lack of control. Social scientists are still trying to determine how much of a person's character is genetically patterned and how much is determined by the environment. Many adopted children who have found their birth parents in later years are surprised to find how much they have in common. In her book, *Parents, Children, and Adoption,* Jane Rowe, Director of the Association of British Adoption Agencies, writes:

> Behavior is much more caught and taught than inherited. . . . The influence of parents and relatives, health or sickness, cultural patterns, education and religious teaching are profound and easily recognized. However, there are limits to which environment can shape the individual. These limits are constitutionally determined.[2]

Instituting Family Fairness
So if each child is genetically different, how do you treat children fairly but distinctly? In families with both biological and adopted children, how do you set rules and privileges which allow equal opportunity and individual consideration? Many parents are overanxious about avoiding the appearance of favoritism, but to a child the most important consideration is not that he is treated identically, but that he is treated fairly.

If Joe loves to fish but Mike doesn't, should their father extend the fishing invitation to both? Yes. If Mike doesn't want to go, however, the father needs to find some sort of activity where he'and Mike can spend time together.

Take the time to understand each child's particular requirements for discipline, love, and attention. As Christ comforts, guides, and disciplines each of us as individuals, so parents must likewise nurture their children on an individual basis.

We Do Not "Own" Our Children
The Bible tells us that children are a heritage of the Lord (Ps. 127:3). Whether biological or adopted, the children that God brings into your life are His property. We are stewards, given the joyous but awesome task of nurturing, training, encouraging, and disciplining these heaven-sent charges. All too soon, children leave the homes in which they were taught and parents find their task has been completed.

It is important for parents to realize that children belong to God. Through this knowledge we can cope with a child's illness or death; lack of this knowledge leaves parents, without Christ, bereft of any comfort when misfortune falls upon their children.

It is also through this principle that we can effectively discipline. We are the caretakers and managers and any power we have to discipline is delegated by God Himself. We ask our children to do right, not because we say so, but because God says so. We are all subject to His authority. Therefore we are to deal wisely and carefully with those eternal souls entrusted to our care.

Seek God's Will before Adopting
When you are feeling the emotional desperation that comes as a result of infertility and everything within you longs for a baby to hold, it is difficult to be emotionally and spiritually. You may be desperately seeking a child without considering that God's plan for you may be to remain childless or simply wait. Be sure God's will for you includes adoption before you move ahead with the option.

Many pastors believe that too often infertile couples seek to adopt a child when they should instead be waiting on the promise of God. The story of Isaac and Ishmael is often used to illustrate the dilemma parents can create when they substitute a child of their own choosing into the role intended for the child of promise. If you feel this is your situation, by all means wait on the Lord. Doctors are not infallible and many women who were once labeled "infertile" do eventually give birth to children.

If I had a dollar for everyone who said to me, "Just wait. As soon as you adopt, you'll get pregnant! The pressure will be off"—I'd have enough money to adopt 10 more kids! Everyone who has told me this knew of someone in this situation; however, doctors tell us that the percentage of women who conceive after adopting a child is no greater than the percentage of women who would have become pregnant anyway. So don't be dissuaded by stories that you hear.

Remember that "infertile" is defined as "unable to conceive a child in one year of unprotected intercourse." Infertile is not the same as *sterile*. Infertile women often do conceive. In fact the Bible records that Isaac, Jacob, Joseph, Samuel, Samson, and John the Baptist were all born of "barren" women. A child who takes some time in coming is truly a special gift from God. With Him, nothing is impossible.

Trust God's Plan and Timing

"But when the fullness of the time was come, God sent forth His Son, made of a woman, made under the law, to redeem them that were under the law, that we might receive the adoption of sons" (Gal. 4:4-5).

I cannot understand why, when a certain fullness of time had come, God sent our children to us. But I do not doubt for one minute that they were meant for us. God's hand was clearly evident in the process. I am always mindful that our God is the One who can take bad things and make them good, ugly situations and make them beautiful.

As we bring up our two adopted beauties in the nurture of the Lord, it is a comfort to know that the most beautiful story in the Bible is a good news adoption tiding: "For God so loved the world, that He gave His only begotten Son that whosoever believeth in Him"—might be adopted! For His example, we are grateful.

TEN
The "Other Mother"

A birth mother is the "other woman" involved in an adoptive relationship. Birth mothers arouse many conflicting emotions within the hearts of the adoptive parent and child. We adoptive parents are thankful they brought our children into the world; we also fear that someday they will intrude on the world we've built. We want to know about the woman who gave birth to our child; at the same time we would like to forget she ever existed. The "other mother" conjures up a variety of feelings and emotions, but without her there would be no children for adoption.

When I think of birth mothers, I think of two women in a land and a culture far removed from my own. One was a 15-year-old orphan who needed to be adopted herself. Did she ever know love, the security of a family, or hope for the future?

The second was a woman involved in a common law marriage, desperately poor with two other children for which she could barely provide. She simply had no means to support a third.

Do these women know how much my world revolves around their flesh and blood? They will probably never know, but I ponder the thought often.

Jo's Story

One day I was surprised by a call from our church's maternity home saying, "There's a girl here who is planning to leave in a few days, but she'd like to tell her story. Are you interested?"

Was I! Aside from being a writer who loves to tell everyone's story, I wanted personally to talk to a girl who could tell me from the other side of the story. I wanted to know what it felt like to make an adoption plan for the baby you had carried for nine months.

I arranged to meet with the girl the next day at two o'clock, after the girls had finished with their school classes. When I walked into the home's office, I saw three girls loitering in the hall. Two were obviously pregnant, one was thin. "Hi," I said. "I'm looking for Jo."

The thin girl smiled. "I'm Jo."

We found a temporarily vacant office and went inside. As I fumbled with the tape recorder, I noticed Jo was pretty in a wholesome, girl-next-door sort of way. She wore a schoolgirl skirt, a plaid blouse, and a blue sweater that matched her sparkling eyes. Her golden brown hair was pulled back into a pony tail and braided, with perky bows tied at the top and bottom. She could have stepped off the cover of *Sixteen;* her countenance was clear and bright.

"Why did you agree to do this?" I wanted to know.

"Well," she paused, "I feel like I accomplished something, and I thought if I can do it, anybody else can do it. I don't think a lot of girls realize that there is an alternative to abortion—I sure didn't at first. But I think it was really good that I did find out about this ministry."

Jo—short for Josephine—was lucky. She heard about the abortion alternative ministry from both her pastor and her grandmother. "My parents didn't find out I was pregnant until I was six and a half months along," she said. "So Daddy called the hotline and we came up here to look over the home. I was here to stay within two weeks."

Jo is a Christian from a Christian family. She attended a Christian school. She knew almost immediately that she was pregnant, but she couldn't bring herself to tell her parents. When she finally did tell them, "For the first time they didn't know how to handle something that had happened to one of us kids. The first night was kind of tough, but after that I knew they'd support me."

Jo's parents felt hurt more than anything. "If it takes kicking you out of the house to make you live up to your responsibility, that's what I'll do," her dad told her. Jo added, "And if that had been the best thing for me, my daddy would have done it."

Did Jo ever consider abortion? "Not really. My boyfriend had given me money for an abortion, but I just kept putting it off. Once I was with another friend whose girlfriend was in the hospital having an abortion. I went with him to sign the papers for the abortion, and I was struck by the depression in that house where all the girls were sitting and waiting to have an abortion. It was just so awful; I never wanted to go through with it."

Jo and her boyfriend broke up after she became pregnant. "I was just so turned off by him that I dumped him. I realize that I made a mistake and he made a mistake. I hope he realizes that he can be forgiven for what we did."

Jo spoke quickly, with a forced breeziness, but she paused when I asked, "What made you decide to make an adoption plan for your baby?"

"Well, I can't be a mother and a father—that just doesn't work. And I know how much my parents have influenced my life, just by being Christian parents. I want to go to college; I already have a lot of things planned for my future. Knowing that my baby will go into a Christian family makes all the difference in the world."

My adoptive parental instincts took over and I couldn't resist asking a few more personal questions. "How do you feel about your baby and—well, obviously you love your baby and want the best for your baby, but tell me how you'll feel in 10 years on his birthday."

Jo did not hesitate. "That was God's baby. I've given it up, and I feel like I've given it up fully. It's not mine anymore and I can't say that I ever felt like it was all mine. It was God's and I was just allowed to carry it for nine months and that's all I can say about him."

Jo's voice quavered and, for the first time, almost broke. "I think that having him . . . was just so neat. I could never forget that."

Whether she needed it or not, I wanted to reassure her. "Jo, as an adoptive parent, let me tell you how I feel about my children. We prayed for them before they came. Although we didn't know it, we prayed for my daughter during the time of her conception and during the nine months before her birth. She is ours in the sense that she is our responsibility to nurture and guide into Christian adulthood. But God used other women to bring my children into this world, and I pray that God will bless those women because they did what they thought was best for those kids."

Jo nodded. I'm sure she had heard it all before.

What advice would Jo give to a pregnant and unmarried girl? "First I'd ask if her parents were Christians, and if they were, I'd urge her to tell them. Also, it's important to confide in a pastor or someone you can trust. Just knowing someone knew about my situation and was praying for me helped me a lot."

Even if a girl's parents are not Christians, she should still be honest with them. Jo knows of many girls who thought their parents would be raving with anger, but instead they rallied around their daughters. Not all parents are understanding, of course, but most are concerned about their unborn grandchildren.

When Jo returns home, she will finish up her junior year in a public school and then she can reenroll in her Christian school for her senior year. "My Christian school principal said he'd be proud to have me graduate from his school," Jo said, smiling. Her family and friends back home have offered nothing but support.

What has Jo learned from this experience? "I think that anybody who goes through anything like this matures a lot. It makes you grow up, and you also grow up a lot spiritually. You have to have someone to lean on, and you can't always rely on your parents because they have to have someone to lean on too. My parents had to have counseling—they just had to have someone to talk to. I think that leaning on God has been good for all of us."

While at the home Jo was impressed by the example of Jill, another girl waiting for her baby to be born. "Jill was really a good Christian, and always was consistent with her daily devotions. That impressed me a lot. The church members here, too, were really great. They treat all the girls well and don't criticize or look down on us. They praise us for not having an abortion and we're not self-conscious in taking a front row seat in church.

Jo had answered all my questions and seemed eager to go outside and talk to the friends she would be leaving in a few days. As I gathered up my notes, I thought that although she seemed older than 16, I could easily picture her giggling at a slumber party or cheering at a high school football game.

She was right. She really had accomplished something, and I was glad. And I knew that somewhere, two adoptive parents were more than glad.

Jo has now faded back into the life from which she came, but I think of her often. She was so young, but so mature, and the child for which she planned is thriving in a Christian home with loving parents.

Remembering Birth Mothers
Columnist Bruce Chapman, writing in the *Wall Street Journal* reminds us that only 50,000 women each year now choose to make an adoption plan for their babies:

> Social agencies and doctors neglect to describe adoption as a practical option, let alone the best one. Young women like you still run an obstacle course to make what is often the best resolution of a difficult problem—the best

for the child, society, and for you—the birth mother. Even if the obstacle course were made an easy path, the adoption option probably would not secure the support it once had. As for media and the entertainment culture, I cannot think of a single positive newspaper or magazine article or television program in recent years describing the perspective of a birth mother who chose placing her child for adoption.

Yet you are remembered. Adoptive parents and their children remember.

We think of you often, and are grateful. So will our son be when he is old enough to understand, for your choice meant survival itself, in the first instance, and then the chance to grow up with two parents in a secure home. It was the right decision for him, and we suspect that it was the right one for you. We think you may be finishing college now, and perhaps you soon will have a family of your own.

When you think back to the first baby you bore, it may be with some sadness. But we hope it is with some satisfaction and pride too, in knowing that you are blessed by at least three people you don't know by name—on Mother's Day.[1]

Not only do adoptive parents appreciate birth mothers who chose adoption over abortion, but adopted children do too. Tracie Gaunt, a student who grew up through our church's youth department, wrote an exceptional letter to the editor of our hometown paper. As her friends and as adoptive parents, we enjoyed reading her words which support the difficult decision of birth mothers:

In a few days I shall celebrate my 18th birthday. I will give thanks to God for several reasons, especially that He has been good to me and blessed me in many ways.

What makes my case unusual, I believe, is that when I was born, my young, unmarried mother decided that I be placed in a childless home. She wasn't able to provide a home for me, but I am thankful she provided an opportunity for me to be raised with love and Christian guidance. I wasn't another number entered in the records at an abortion clinic.

No doubt it was less convenient for my biological mother to have carried me for the full term of the pregnancy. It would have been more convenient for her had she chosen the easy way out—abortion. I am glad she was willing to endure the inconvenience in order that I might have life.

Today some things haven't changed. Young mothers are faced with a problem: they can carry a young life in their body, but can't provide a home for that child. Too many will choose the "discreet, quick and quiet" solution—a visit to the abortion clinic. Another situation hasn't changed—the choice of seeing that the child is placed in a home where there is love, guidance, and Christian upbringing.

I would hope that anyone who might read this letter and who might face similar circumstances, as my biological mother did, would think of my situation. Thank God she chose life for me.[2]

A Difficult Choice

Annice Craddock is a special woman and a friend. In 1985 she and her husband, John, decided to help pregnant girls. The Craddocks established the Love Life Maternity Home in Florence, South Carolina, and today Love Life offers education, medical help, living quarters, and adoption services for interested girls.

When a baby is born at Love Life, the birth mother has a free choice whether to keep the child or make an adoption plan. For those who choose adoption, Annice is loving and sympathetic. "I go through labor and delivery with all my girls," explains Annice. "When the baby is born I hold him up so my girl can examine all his fingers and toes. I tell the girl, 'Thank you for giving this baby life.' I have one small baby in one arm and a big baby in the other, and we all huddle together and cry. It's very hard to give up something you've had within you for nine months."

One birth mother wrote the following unsigned letter to *National Right to Life News*. Like the young women at Love Life, she made a difficult decision and faced it with bravery and determination:

> I remember pulling into the hospital parking lot noticing the emptiness and darkness. I hurt a lot and was so frightened. One of those silly thoughts came over me amidst all the gloom—I wondered if I had enough change on me for the parking meter.
>
> It was almost four a.m. and the main corridor of the hospital seemed so bright. I found a nurse and told her I thought my baby was due to be born. I was 28 years old and didn't live near my family. I never told them I had a baby—to this day.
>
> All during the pregnancy not an hour would go by that I didn't argue with myself in regard to keeping the baby and/or adoption. In one breath I kept saying that I'll fight and scrape and work two jobs to keep him. Then reality would set in and I knew I didn't have an education, or any money, or a husband. What a selfish thing it would be to do to this baby of mine who deserved so much.
>
> I kept contacting an adoption agency, wanting to know their procedures. Looking back, I think I knew deep down he would have a better chance. I just kept hoping I could find a better way.
>
> Well, the nurse insisted I sit in the wheelchair. I actually argued with her. It was too final. I would have to make a decision.
>
> It was 1967. I knew nothing of politics, was not reli-

giously inclined, had no direction in my life, but was positive from the very beginning that I was carrying a child.

The next morning with only God knowing how lost I felt and that I was giving up the only good thing I had going for me, I decided to give my baby to someone else. At least he would have a home and a father.

It's been 14 years and I have since met, married, and birthed (two beauties). Remembering the tears that flowed over the kind lady's desk, over the adoption papers, and over me for days afterward, I still believe it was the right thing for me at the time.

Now I read where they are relaxing the rules for adopted children to meet their birth mothers. Why would I adopt my child out when it would be almost a sure bet he'd be back in 18 years? Particularly if I felt that what I did, by the adoption, was the safest thing for both of us.

On the other hand, would I adopt a child and put in a good 18 years of love and anguish only to find that my son wants to see his mother and could do so with relative ease?

If my child needs medical information, I will gladly help. And, lo and behold, if he comes knocking on my door in a few years I'll not deny him. But I will never agree with opening those files. I signed those papers with the understanding that that part of my life was going to be private then, now, and always.

I think of my baby now and then, and through the years on his birthday I silently wish him well. I don't fall apart like some social-do-gooders think I should. They make it sound like a requirement.

If there is anything I can say that I'm proud of in the whole ordeal, it's that I can stand a little straighter because I gave my child life.[3]

Not only do birth mothers endure pain, torment, and the stress of a difficult decision, but they also lose their privacy. "The legalization of abortion meant that young girls could make a confidential decision to terminate their pregnancy," Bill Pierce, director of the National Committee for Adoption, told *Christianity Today.* "No one except the doctor knows."[4]

On the other hand, that same right of privacy is not extended to girls who choose to carry their babies to term. Title IX of the education law requires school districts to "mainstream" a pregnant girl into regular classes, and unless she is one of the fortunate ones who find an opening in a maternity home, she must attend school with a bulging belly. There are no private tutors and no privacy. If a girl doesn't want everybody to know and wants to continue her education, she is left with only one option: abortion.

"There's a lot of peer pressure in schools," says Pierce. "Kids say things like, 'If you didn't want to keep it you'd have had an abortion, right? Who would give away their own flesh and blood?' "[5]

Who indeed? Only the few, the proud, the brave—the birth mothers.

ELEVEN
The Future of Adoption

Taryn Li arrived in our arms on November 4, 1983. We completed our six-month trial period, went to visit the lawyer, and waited for the paperwork to travel from desk to desk in our state's social service system. Finally on October 26, 1984, I received the letter than her adoption had been finalized. We were a legal family.

Only a few days later my husband and I were trying to decide how we could sell our house, finance another adoption, and find room for another son or daughter. We set out on faith, put our house on the market, and called our friendly local social worker, Helen.

The second time around seemed to be much easier. We knew what to expect and we were good friends with the social workers. We set up an appointment with Helen to update our home study and during our single one-hour visit, we talked about how life with Taryn had changed us, what our extended families were up to, and how Iowa State was doing in football. Taryn ransacked the room as we talked, and I began to be excited about the prospect of having a little brother to keep her company.

Helen explained that our file would be reopened in the state office, we would have to have another physical examination, and once again we would have to provide references. We plunged in again, as eager as before, but not as anxious. This time I knew God's timing would be perfect and the time we spent waiting would only be one of preparation for our new child, for us, and for Taryn.

It took nearly a month for the reference letters to return to Helen and she was so swamped with work that it was several months before our home study update was sent to our international agency in Washington, D.C. But soon after our Washington social worker received our update, she called. Would we like to come to Washington to look at the papers of another baby? Of course!

We had just moved and the new house was in total chaos, but we would come within the week. Before Mary hung up I hesitantly asked, "Mary—can you tell me? Is it a boy or a girl?"

I could hear the smile in her voice as she replied, "He's a very nice little boy. Born on August 21—he's five months old." When Gary came home, I greeted him: "Congratulations, Dad. You're about to have a son!"

We left early for Washington the next week and found our agency's office after driving aimlessly through the sprawling city for over an hour. Taryn loved wandering through the offices and Gary and I were delighted to see Mary again. After we had seated ourselves across from her desk, she handed us a biographical sketch of a little boy who had been placed in a foundling home at two days of age. He was tiny, frail, and his photographs showed a worried frown puckering his delicate features. We quickly scanned the report and exclaimed, "We'll take him!"

"Not so quickly," said Mary. "He has a medical condition—a hemangioma on his forehead. I want you to go and get something to eat, talk about it, and come back before you give me an answer."

We asked her about the hemangioma—we had never heard of it. It was a birthmark, actually a benign tumor of tiny blood vessels that clump together while the baby is being formed in the womb. This child's hemangioma was located on his forehead, between his brows. Perhaps it would fade with time, perhaps it would not. It made no difference to us.

At lunch we talked about everything but the birthmark. We returned and told Mary again, "We'll take him."

She warned us, "This is not a perfect child."

"We're not perfect parents," I interrupted. We proceeded to fill out the necessary forms for the acceptance, gave him his new name, and we left hoping that in six weeks or so Tyler Jordan Hunt would be coming home.

Six weeks and two days later we were back at Washington National Airport anxiously anticipating the delivery of our son. After his six-month probationary period, he legally became a part of our family on March 4, 1986. We used a different lawyer for Tyler's adoption and were thrilled when he called to tell us we were to appear before the judge for the finalization. Lovers of ceremony, we dressed carefully and made sure Taryn and Tyler made it from their bedrooms to the car without encountering mud, drool, or grape juice. We arrived in the lawyer's office, entertained the children for half an hour in his waiting room, and then walked down the street to the judge's chambers.

I'm glad we did Tyler's finalization in court because at least we can say we did one adoption with ceremony. If I add a little dramatic flair it will make a nice story for my son in the future, but honestly, my most striking memory of that day is how the cobblestone sidewalks outside the courthouse hurt my feet in my too-tight high heels. I don't think Tyler or Taryn will remember anything.

We entered the judge's chambers, which did not resemble any of the lavish oaken offices I've seen on television, and sat in a row of chairs at the back of the room. Twenty feet away, the judge sat at his desk and our lawyer routinely handed him our papers. The judge quickly signed them with hardly a glance at their content. When the last paper was signed, the judge glanced up at us for the first time, smiled and remarked that we looked like a happy family—we replied that we were—

and the grand ceremony was done. A week later I received Tyler's birth certificate in the mail.

How Many Kids Should You Adopt?

How many more times do we plan to adopt? I don't know. I don't feel that my family is complete, but financial circumstances and time constraints of the future may limit our emotional desire to "adopt a dozen kids." Other mothers laugh and tell me they definitely know when they've had one child too many, but we will just wait and see.

I met my friend, Jan Reber, in the drug store recently. Jan is a beautiful mother to five girls and she must have been surprised when I blurted out, "Jan, is having five kids worth it? I mean, I know the older ones help with the smaller ones and they learn responsibility, but really—is it too difficult?"

Her gentle brown eyes smiled at my honest confusion. "Angie, just remember one thing: your children are the only things on earth you can take to heaven with you."

Suddenly I wished for a hundred kids. Oh, I know I can't literally take them to heaven with me, but I can certainly do my best to lead them to a knowledge of Christ and His provision for salvation.

Other parents have felt the same way. John and Mary Ann Kuharski were attending a Marriage Encounter retreat when someone asked, "Do you think you have all the children God intends for you to have?" At that time the Kuharskis had four children, two biological and two adopted, but felt God might have more in mind for them. One by one more children were added, through birth and by adoption, until today the Kuharskis, at last count, had twelve children, seven teenagers, three school-age children, and two toddlers.

Mary Ann Kuharski writes:

Having a dozen kids is certainly not for everyone, but we clearly believe this was God's plan and our fulfilled vocation. No matter how tight our budget has been, there has always been somebody to help. We received unexpected raises, a gift from a dying uncle and a thoughtful present from a neighbor. We've learned to live on faith and in the process, we've seen that God is never outdone in generosity. Any sacrifices on our part have been more than compensated for in other ways.

Still, I would be lying if I painted a completely happy-ever-after picture. We have had more than our share of sorrows, losses, and tears—perhaps more than a small family can ever imagine. Just our sheer number, diversity of backgrounds and personalities, emotional scars and adjustments, could keep a team of Mayo Clinic psychologists busy for months. There's been more failure and heartache than we ever thought possible. Yet our laughter, joy, and love more than offsets those occasionally blue days.[1]

In Cedar Falls, Iowa, another American family has found its existence through adoption. Jim and Jody Swarbrick have 16 children (and counting), all but one of whom were adopted. Before the children were adopted, they were carefully described to the Swarbricks, but many did not live up to their descriptions. Luke, nine, and Andy, seven, were Korean orphans who, according to a social worker, might "lie, cheat, steal, swear, or run wild." The boys got off the plane and bowed respectfully to their new parents. Joey, six, was described as having cerebral palsy, but after he was home his family eventually learned he had muscular dystrophy. Joey learned to walk, attended kindergarten, and never missed an episode of Kung Fu Theater. He died at home at age nine.[2]

Tony and Karen Insua, of central Florida, had four biological children when they watched a television special on Vietnamese-American children. Their hearts were stirred, so they checked out international adoption but found the large fees discouraging. The Insuas called the Florida Department of Health and Rehabilitative Services and found that there were hundreds of waiting children in the state of Florida. These were not "healthy, white infants," but all were in desperate need of a home.

Commitment, patience, love, and faith in God are the most important keys to adjustment, says Tony Insua. "The most important thing to remember about adjustment problems is that they are temporary."

Today the Insuas have 10 children ranging in age from 3 to 19. The children love and respect each other, but most of all, they have learned to share. The couple's strength is their faith in God. They told a reporter for a local newspaper, "The Bible says prosperity and children go together."[3]

Just as there are couples who fall in love with adoption and plan to adopt as many as possible, there are other families who are completely satisfied and content with one or two children. "It really doesn't matter whether the children are adopted or not," one mother told me; "it just depends on your family's lifestyle and whether or not you can mentally and emotionally handle a large family. I want my two kids to have piano lessons, ballet lessons, a nice home, and a Christian education, and we simply can't afford to do all of those things for more than two kids."

The Future of Adoption

Whether you would like to adopt 1 child or 10, will you be able to in the future? What is the future of adoption in this country?

Many prospective parents are concerned about the trend toward "open adoption." This type of adoption, where a child is placed in a home where the adoptive parents have either met or received identifying information about the biological parents, is receiving much attention in the media. Many adoptive parents and relinquishing mothers have expressed concern over the loss of confidentiality which open adoption proposes. Just how close are we to mandatory open adoption? No one knows for sure, but many agencies and courts alike are wary of this experiment.

On a "Donahue" show which centered around adoption, an adoptive mother of five children pointed out that if open adoption were legalized, she would co-parent with 5 other sets of parents and 10 additional sets of grandparents. Is this the foundation for emotional stability and family security?

Yet, as the supply of infants grows shorter, biological mothers realize they have more input into the future home of their baby. A program sponsored by Catholic Social Services in Brevard County, Florida, introduces adoptive parents and birth mothers. "It's all confidential," said Jo Williams, a social worker with the Catholic Social Services, "There's no sharing of last names or addresses." She believes that the program relieves fears of both the adoptive parents and the birth mother. The birth mother is reassured that her baby will be with loving parents; the adoptive parents see the biological mother as a person with deep feelings. They also gain information that their child may want to know later.[4]

Other "open adoption" programs encourage more contact. The birth mother may often visit the child throughout the years and grow to be a friend of the family. But many experts disagree with such openness. Richard Zeilinger, executive director of the Children's Bureau of New Orleans, says that confidentiality protects the stability of the new adoptive family. "Once you put that wedge in the door, it gets wider and wider," he says. "In the long run, it destroys adoption."[5]

In May 1985 Jodi Johnson broke up with her boyfriend and discovered she was pregnant. Three days over the legal limit for an abortion, she followed her mother's urging and placed her baby for adoption. Jodi agreed, as long as she could be assured she wouldn't lose sight of her baby forever. She placed her baby with a family which supported open adoption.

After spending four days with her baby, Jodi arranged for the adoptive family to pick up the baby. She visited with them three times during the baby's first year, and visits occasionally even now. But she doesn't telephone and she does exhibit mature behavior. Kathleen Silber believes Jodi's response is typical of birth mothers involved in open adoption: "Most go back to their own lives immensely relieved and, therefore, less obsessed with what has happened to their babies."[6]

Although open adoption may ease a biological mother's mind and dispel the "need to search" in the adoptees, the process is new and has not been tested. What if, in the years to come, the birth mother sees something in the family she doesn't like? What if the child becomes confused about which woman is his real, emotional mother? What role will the biological grandparents play? Open adoption is replete with possibilities for disaster.

Open Adoption Records

Open adoption should not be confused with open adoption *records*. There are basically four different legal positions regarding adoption records: open records, search and consent, the registry concept, and confidential records. Presently there are only two states with open records, Alabama and Kansas. *Open records* allows any adult adoptee to simply pay a small fee and receive his original birth certificate on demand.

In states with a *search and consent* provision, an adoptee who would like to meet his biological parents can contact the state and make known his wishes. The state will then contact the biological parents, and if they agree, a meeting can be arranged. If they do not agree, the information is withheld from the adoptee.

A *registry* can involve two or three parties—the adoptee, the biological parents, and the adoptive parents. When all of the necessary parties enter into the registry, the information is released so that a meeting can be arranged. Most people who support this concept would also require that the adoptee be at least eighteen years of age.

States which have a *confidential records* policy will not release any information unless instructed to do so by a direct court order. For more information about adoption records laws, contact your state office of the Bureau of Vital Statistics.

One group pressing for open adoption records, Adoptees in Search, claims that sealed birth records violate their natural rights granted by the First, Fifth, Ninth, Thirteenth, and Four-teenth Amendments to the Constitution. These people want to have the freedom to find their birth mothers, but Margot Joan Fromer makes an interesting point about open adoption in her article, "My Mother Deserves to Remain Anonymous:"

> There's nothing essentially wrong with this, but what I find selfishly insupportable is their belief that it is accept-able to translate a personal desire into rights language and to term a promise of anonymity made to the birth mother an "antiquated social concern." One cannot claim a right to something simply because one wants it. More-over, one cannot ignore that the birth mother has a con-tinuing right to count on that legally granted anonymity."[7]

The "reunion" movement is advancing primarily because of medical advances which allow, for instance, organ-transplant patients to fare far better with biologically related donors. James Woytowicz, of Massachusetts, needed a blood relative to donate bone marrow to combat his leukemia. His birth mother was found and insisted on anonymity although she was willing to donate bone marrow if he needed it.

Her refusal to meet did not affect Woytowicz. "I needed to contact her for health reasons," he told *Parade* magazine, "not to reclaim a mother. My mother is Stefania Woytowicz, the woman who raised me since I was two months old. I think what my birth mother is doing is being done out of her heart. She's willing to give me part of her body. She deserves to have her identity protected."[8]

Other Adoption Trends
The future of adoption is uncertain and ever changing. I'd be

foolish to try to guess what lies ahead on the adoption scene, but there are some trends worth noting.

The following situation is exceptionally unusual, but it illustrates what I believe will be a trend for agencies in being completely honest about the children they place for adoption. In January 1988, the *Los Angeles Times* reported that a Santa Ana couple had agreed to accept $70,000 from Orange County, California rather than continue their lawsuit against its Social Services agency.

The couple, Tom and Janice Colella, had waited for more than four years before adoption officials called to tell them they had a son: a beautiful, all-American seven-year-old. The forms they signed with their case worker stated the county had no medical information on their son beyond the fact that he was born with rickets, had a severe bronchial infection shortly after birth, and a broken collarbone in 1976.

The Colellas say they were told the boy was a "misunderstood child" whose adjustment problems could easily be overcome with love and guidance.

The boy, however, attacked his new mother within a week of his adoption. Before his adoption was finalized he killed his hamster and mutilated the ear of the family dog.

After time and investigation, the Colellas found that the boy had been relinquished by his birth mother when he was five years old because, among other reasons, he had set fire to their home. The child was diagnosed as suffering from fetal alcohol syndrome and was placed in two foster homes where his bizarre, violent behavior was noted.

Before their difficult situation ended, the Colellas had endured the boy's suicide attempt, his confinement to a state hospital for 16 months, death threats against them, and expenses of over $300,000 for psychiatric care. When it became clear the young man had problems which the couple was not equipped to handle, they decided to ask that the adoption be voided. When their attorney obtained the complete county files on the child, the couple was so upset by the amount of information withheld from them, they decided to sue.

"We want to tell people who are adopting children that they have to be really careful," Mrs. Colella told a *Los Angeles Times* reporter. "They should get a court order to release all documents on the child to them. I think that at least our efforts have made a change in the system, which is hard to do."[9]

The Colella's situation is exceptionally unusual, and the typical couple who is adopting should not fear that they will adopt a psychopath. But a careful social worker will investigate the backgrounds of the birth parents and the child, and there should be no surprises.

Other trends in adoption include a concern with the number of children available. The National Committee for Adoption estimated that in 1985 over 2 million infertile couples sought to adopt healthy white newborns, but only 25,000 of them were successful.[10]

The shortage of healthy white infants continues and probably will unless a legislative effort radically changes the easy availability of abortion in this country. In the minute it takes you to read one page in this book, three babies are killed by abortion in the United States: 1.5 million each year.[11] Court decisions upholding the rights of fathers have paradoxically made adoption difficult. A 1985 report by the National Committee for Adoption says, "It is ironic that while a woman can unilaterally choose a confidential abortion, she does not have the unilateral right to place the child for adoption.[12]

Newsweek magazine reported in April, 1986 that two opposite factions, however, have agreed that adoption is a crucial issue. Both pro-life and pro-abortion forces have realized there is a need to better inform pregnant women about the adoption option. The Rocky Mountain chapter of Planned Parenthood held a conference to discuss adoption services. "We haven't been convinced that adoption has been presented as a real, positive choice," acting director Sylvia Clark told *Newsweek*.[13]

The pro-abortion forces even believe that promoting adoption may help disintegrate opposition to abortion. "What better way to splinter the opposition?" says Dr. Frank Bonati, who operates the only federally funded family-planning agency that offers adoption services. "No mother is going to get out and picket an agency that provided her with a baby."[14]

A clinic in San Antonio offers both abortion and adoption services under one roof. Rather than turn away women with advanced pregnancies who are ineligible for abortion, counselors ask women if they would be willing to make an adoption plan for their babies. "With less than 5 percent of unwed American mothers willing to put their children up for adoption," says a writer for *Time*, "the small number of women who cross the boundary from abortion clinic to adoption service may seem like a bonanza to childless couples."[15]

In 1987 President Reagan appointed a task force to "expand and broaden our efforts to make sure that America's family-less children are adopted." Reagan said, "We must do all we can to remove obstacles that prevent qualified adoptive parents from accepting these children into their homes." The Reagan administration expressed interest in presenting adoption to women who are considering raising a child alone or obtaining an abortion.[16]

But even if the availability of white, healthy infants grows, prospective parents should look to the other children available. Hundreds of children who wait in the United States can be placed at no expense to the parents.

Is there any tax relief for adoptive parents? Although adopted children are classified as dependents, as of this writing adoption expenses are not tax deductable unless the child is an American special-needs adoption (and this may be threatened with the tax law changes of 1988 and beyond). Four states, however, currently allow tax deductions for adoption expenses: California, Massachusetts, Wisconsin, and Minnesota.

There Are Children Who Wait
Every other month when I receive my copy of *Ours* magazine, I turn quickly to the pages where the "waiting children" are featured. I see pictures of darling children who want and

need to be loved, and it is hard to resist calling my social worker.

"Anna Rosa (Brazil), nine, is a robust, happy girl who gets along well with everyone and especially does well in school. Without the encouragement a family can give, Anna Rosa has completed several grades and is in the equivalent of the U.S. fifth grade. Her smile would brighten any home!"[17]

"Fatima, born ten years ago, is a slender, petite girl. Her young sister has found a forever home in Brazil and Fatima is fearful there is no family for her. She has explicitly told her Judge that she wants a family now! Fatima is an average student whose work has been prejudiced by the disruption of her family."[18]

"Han Dae Ho is an adoptable five-year-old who has waited for too long in Korea for a family of his own. Two years ago Dae Ho was burned on his back side from his waist to the bottom of his buttocks by hot water. His keloid scars itch, especially at night time. This very bright little boy expresses himself well in every way. He says that when he grows up he wants to be a 'doctor who will cure patients.' "[19]

"The family—Johnny, ten years; Frank, nine years; Evelin, seven years; Vanessa, five years; and Pier, three years. They were found in a state of abandonment and are being cared for in a welfare institution. They all have normal physical and mental health. They have adapted to the institution; however, they are beginning to show evidence of emotional and educational deprivation. The Child Welfare Institution prefers one family, as they have a close relationship; or two families within the same area would be considered."[20]

There are so many children with such great needs. The children come from every corner of the earth, in every imaginable shade, shape, and size. Their histories all differ, but they share a vital need in common: to have a forever family, a place to find love, security, and a sense of belonging. Won't you consider one of these children for your family?

Notes

Chapter 1: Why Consider Adoption?

1. Janis Johnson, "Most Infertility Can Be Conquered," *USA Today* (May 11, 1983), p. 30.
2. For practical advice, read *How To Get Pregnant* by Dr. Sherman Silber. See *Suggested Reading* list.
3. Tom Seligson, "Wanted: A Permanent Home," *Parade* (July 31, 1988), p. 5.
4. Bruce Chapman, "Happy Birth-mother's Day," *Wall Street Journal* (May 10, 1985), p. OP-ED.
5. Maryann Bucknum Brinley, "The Baby Business," *McCall's* (June 1985), pp. 89ff.
6. "Where Are the Babies?" *Parents* (November 1987), p. 176.
7. Bonnie Johnson, "Mr. Stork Delivers," *People* (April 21, 1986), pp. 78-85.
8. For more information, write to Resolve, Inc., P.O. Box 474, Belmont, Mass. 02178 or telephone them at (617) 484-2424.
9. Stephanie Azzarone, "New Options in Adoptions," *Money* (November 1981), p. 92.
10. Rochelle Distelheim, "The Boundless Love of Keith and Sharon Gill," *McCall's* (July 1985), p. 66ff.
11. Personal interview with Jack and Rexella Van Impe, October 31, 1986.

Chapter 2: Where Are the Children?

1. Phone interview with Jeff Rosenburg of the National Committee for Adoption, July 29, 1988.
2. Alicia Shepard, "Adoption Scams," *St. Petersburg Times* (December 6, 1987).
3. Associated Press, "Baby Chase Follows Climbing Demand for Adoptions," *News and Daily Advance*, Lynchburg, Virginia (June 14, 1987).
4. *Ibid.*
5. For more information and detailed reports on the laws regarding independent adoptions in each of the 50 states, read the *Adoption Factbook*. See *Suggested Reading* list.
6. Check the *Adoption Factbook* (see above) for agencies to contact in your state. A partial list of private agencies is included at the end of this book under *Agency Listings*.
7. Adapted from "Shopping for an Adoption Agency—A Consumer's Guide," Forever Families, P.O. Box 433, Bellevue, WA 98009; and Cindy Savage and Kathy Zamboni, "Considerations in Selecting an Adoption Agency," *Ours* (January/February 1986), p. 7.
8. Order from the Immigration and Naturalization Service, 25 E. St. N.W., Washington, D.C. 20538. The cost is $1.75.

9. The National Adoption Hotline, (202-463-7563), can also give you information about adoption in general or international adoption in particular. You may wish to write the Hotline sponsor, the National Committee for Adoption, Suite 326, 1346 Connecticut Avenue, N.W., Washington, D.C. 20036.

Chapter 4: What Kind of Child for You?

1. Associated Press, "Mother's Love Stretches to Ends of Earth," *Florida Today* (May 10, 1987).
2. Claudia Jewett, *Adopting the Older Child* (Harvard, Mass.: The Harvard Common Press, 1978), p. 5.
3. *Ibid.*, p. 14.
4. *Ibid.*
5. Jane Marks, "We Have a Problem," *Parents* (October 1987), p. 62.
6. Lynn Norment, "One Church/One Child," *Ebony* (March 1986), p. 68.
7. Walter Leavy, "Should Whites Adopt Black Children?" *Ebony* (September 1987), p. 78.
8. *Ibid.*
9. Evelyn West Ayrault, *Growing Up Handicapped* (N.Y.: Seabury Press, 1977).
10. Associated Press, "Couple Adopts Handicapped Children Along with Problems," *News and Daily Advance*, Lynchburg, Virginia (April 13, 1986).
11. Patricia Caporale, "Taking a Chance on Love," *Ladies' Home Journal* (May 1987), pp. 22ff.
12. Personal interview with Nancy Rockwood, January 1986.
13. Taken from "Special Needs Adoption," *Children Today* (September/October 1984), pp. 3-5.
14. Rita Laws, "It's Time to Notice Our Invisible Children," *U.S. News and World Report* (August 10, 1987), p. 4.

Chapter 5: International Adoptions

1. "Where Are the Babies?" *Parents* (November 1987), p. 176.
2. Karla Reynolds, "Dispelling Fears," *Ours* (November/December 1987), p. 6.
3. Jerry Ann Jenista, M.D., "Update: AIDS," *Ours* (November/December 1987), p. 29.
4. To receive an updated ICCC list and informational brochure send $15.00 to:
   International Concerns Committee for Children
   911 Cypress Drive
   Boulder, CO 80303

5. For more information contact OURS at:
   OURS, Inc.
   3307 Highway 100 North, Suite 203
   Minneapolis, MN 55422

(612) 535-4829
Helpline: (612) 434-4930

Chapter 6: The Wait

1. Mary Ann Kuharski, "Something More in Store," *Focus on the Family* (November 1987), p. 6.
2. There are also support groups for couples struggling with infertility (RESOLVE has chapters throughout the country; call (617) 484-2424 for more information) and families who have adopted foreign children (FACE: Families Adopting Children Everywhere has many local chapters).

Chapter 7: Facing the Public

1. Rita Laws, "Four Adoption Laws Defined," *Ours* (May/June 1986), p. 25.
2. Linda Caughey, letter to editor, *Ours* (November/December 1987), p. 7.
3. Patricia Irwin Johnson, "Addressing the Ostrich Syndrome," *Ours* (January/February 1986), pp. 8-9.
4. *Ibid.*

Chapter 8: Your New Child at Home

1. I recommend two books, both by T. Berry Brazelton, *Infants and Mothers* (NY: Dell Publishing, 1969) and *To Listen to a Child* (Reading, Mass.: Addison-Wesley Publishing Company, 1984).
2. Candace E. Wheeler, *Moving In: Adopting Older Children* (Juneau, Alaska: Winking Owl Press, 1978), pp. 5-6.
3. Alfred A. Messer, "A Doctor's Rx for Easing Adoption Pain," *Wall Street Journal* (April 29, 1985).
4. Roberta Plutzik, "The Special Passages of Adopted Children," *Family Weekly* (February 28, 1983), p. 17.
5. Valentina P. Wasson, *The Chosen Baby*, trans. Glo Coalson (New York: Lippincott Junior Books, 1977).
6. Plutzik, "Special Passages," p. 17.
7. Kelsey Menehan, "The Making of a Sudden Family," *Today's Christian Woman* (May 1987), p. 13.
8. Ann Iivery, "Adopted . . . and Special," *National Right to Life News* (October 28, 1982), p. 5.
9. Wheeler, *Moving In*, p. 24.
10. Personal interview with Dr. Clyde Narramore, Lynchburg, Virginia, April 28, 1986.
11. *Ibid.*

Chapter 9: How Does God View Adoption?

1. Harold Willmington, *Willmington's Guide to the Bible* (Wheaton, IL: Tyndale House, 1981), pp. 735-36.
2. Jane Rowe, *Parents, Children and Adoption: A Handbook for Adoption*

Workers (London: Routledge and Kegan Paul, 1966), n.p.

Chapter 10: The Other Mother

1. Bruce Chapman, "Happy Birthmother's Day," *Wall Street Journal* (May 10, 1985).
2. Tracie Gaunt, *Lynchburg News and Daily Advance*, n.d.
3. Unsigned letter, *National Right to Life News* (October 28, 1982), p. 6.
4. Kelsey Menehan, "Where Have All the Babies Gone?" *Christianity Today* (October 18, 1985), p. 28.
5. *Ibid.*

Chapter 11: The Future of Adoption

1. Mary Ann Kuharski, "Something More in Store," *Focus on the Family* (November 1987), pp. 6-7.
2. Alan Richman, "You Mustn't Miss Las Vegas, Mikhail," *People* (August 4, 1986), p. 82.
3. Jeanne Diener, "All in the Family," *The News Chief,* Winter Haven, FL (November 23, 1986).
4. Alice Moynihan, "Adoption Option," *Tribune,* Cocoa, Florida.
5. Barbara Kantrowitz with Elisa Williams, "Life with Two Mothers," *Newsweek* (May 12, 1986), p. 86.
6. Rochelle Distelheim, "Two Mothers for Laura," *McCalls* (September 1987), pp. 135-37.
7. Margot Joan Fromer, "My Mother Deserves to Remain Anonymous," *Washington Post* (October 31, 1982).
8. Bernard Gavzer, "Who Am I?" *Parade* (October 27, 1985), p. 26.
9. Dianne Klein, "Adoption Nightmare," *Los Angeles Times,* reprinted in the *St. Petersburg Times* (January 5, 1988).
10. Elisa Williams, Peter McKillop, and Diane Weathers, "Adoption vs. Abortion," *Newsweek* (April 28, 1986), p. 39.
11. Kelsey Menehan, "Where Have All the Babies Gone?" *Christianity Today* (October 18, 1985), p. 28.
12. "How Can Government Encourage Adoption?" *Christianity Today* (October 2, 1987), p. 54.
13. Williams, McKillop, and Weathers, "Adoption," p. 39.
14. *Ibid.*
15. "Abort/Adopt," *Time* (November 2, 1987), p. 60.
16. Williams, McKillop, and Weathers, "Adoption," p. 53.
17. "Waiting Children," *Ours* (January/February 1986), p. 37.
18. *Ibid.*
19. *Ibid.*, p. 43.
20. "Waiting Children," *Ours* (July/August 1985), p. 28.

Suggested Reading

Books which are currently out of print may be found at your library. Many can be ordered from the National Committee for Adoption, OURS, or from other distributors. Addresses have been given where applicable.

Infertility

Glass, Robert H. and Ronald J. Ericsson. *Getting Pregnant in the 1980's*. Los Angeles: University of California Press, 1982.

"Infertility, Childlessness, and You," pamphlet published by the National Committee for Adoption.*

Menning, Barbara E. *Infertility: A Guide for the Childless Couple*. National Committee for Adoption.*

"The Psychological Dimensions of Infertility," reprint available through the National Committee for Adoption.*

Silber, Sherman J. *How to Get Pregnant*. New York: Warner Books, 1981.

Van Regenmorter, John and Sylvia, and Joe S. McIlhaney, Jr., M.D. *Dear God, Why Can't We Have a Baby?* Grand Rapids: Baker Books, 1986.

For Prospective Adoptive Parents

Adamec, Chris. *There ARE Babies to Adopt*. Lexington, Mass.: Mills and Sanderson, 1987.

Bumgarner, Norma J. *Helping Love Grow: Some Hints for Mothering Your Adopted Baby*. Franklin Park, Illinois: La Leche League, 1974.

Carney, Ann. *No More Here and There: Adopting the Older Child*. North Carolina: University of North Carolina Press, 1976.

Gilman, Lois. *The Adoption Resource Book*. New York: Harper and Row, 1984.

The Immigration and Naturalization Service. *The Immigration of Adopted and Prospective Adoptive Children*. Washington, D.C. May be ordered from the Service at the Department of Justice, 25 E Street N.W., Washington, D.C. 20538. Cost is $1.75.

Jewett, Claudia L. *Adopting the Older Child*. Harvard, Mass.: The Harvard Common Press, 1978.

———. *Helping Children Cope with Separation and Loss*. Boston: Harvard Common Press, 1982.

Katz, Sanford, William Meezan, and Evan Manoff Russo. *Adoptions Without Agencies*. New York: Child Welfare League of America, Inc., 1978.

Kempe, R.S. and C. H. *Child Abuse*. Cambridge, Mass.: Harvard University Press, 1978.

Klibanoff, Susan and Elton. *Let's Talk About Adoption*. Boston: Little, Brown, and Company, 1973.

Ladner, Joyce. *Mixed Families*. Garden City, N.Y.: Doubleday, 1977.

Lindsay, Jeanne Warren. *Open Adoption: A Caring Option*. Buena Park, CA: Morning Glory Press, 1987. (Order from the publisher, 6595-G San Haroldo Way, Buena Park, CA 90620. Also has a study and discussion guide available.)

Magid, Kenneth and Carole A. McKelvey. *High Risk: Children Without A Conscience*. New York: Bantam Books, 1988.

Martin, Cynthia D. *Beating the Adoption Game*. San Diego: Oaktree Publications, 1980.

National Committee for Adoption. *Adoption Factbook*. Washington, D.C. This is the first book you should buy if you are serious about adoption. It includes lists of member agencies, state-by-state parent support groups, state adoption specialists, information on single-parent, international, and interracial adoption, and much more. Send $20.80 to the National Committee for Adoption, P.O. Box 33366, Washington, D.C. 20033.*

The North American Council on Adoptable Children. *Self-Awareness, Self-Selection, and Success*. Minneapolis, MN. To receive this parent preparation guidebook for special needs adoptions send $8.00 to the Council at P.O. Box 14808, Minneapolis, MN 55414.

Plumez, Jacqueline Hornor. *Successful Adoption: A Guide to Finding a Child and Raising a Family*. New York: Crown Publishers, 1982.

Ours Magazine, 3307 Hwy. 100 North, Minneapolis, MN 55422.

Silber, Kathleen and Phylis Speedlin. *Dear Birthmother, Thank You for Our Baby*. San Antonio, TX: Corona Publishing Conpany, 1982.

Smith, Dorothy W. and Laurie Nehls Sherwen. *Mothers and Their Adopted Children: The Bonding Process*. New York: The Tiresias Press, Inc., 1983.

Smith, Jerome and Franklin Miroff. *You're Our Child*. Lanham, Maryland: University Press of America, 1981.

Strom, Kay Marshall. *Chosen Families*. Grand Rapids, Michigan: Zondervan Publishing House, 1985.

The Womanly Art of Breast-Feeding. Franklin Park, Illinois: La Leche International, 1981.

Wheeler, Candace. *Moving In: Adopting Older Children*, Juneau, Alaska: The Winking Owl Press, 1978.

Books for Adopted Children

Caines, Jeannette. *Abby.* New York: Harper and Row, 1973 (for preschoolers).

Krementz, Jill. *How It Feels to Be Adopted.* New York: Knopf Publishers, 1982 (for older children).

Livingston, Carole. *Why Was I Adopted?* Secaucus, New Jersey: Lyle Stuart Publishers, 1978.

Paterson, Katherine. *The Great Gilly Hopkins,* New York: Harper and Row, 1978.

Tax, Meredith. *Families.* Boston: Little, Brown, and Company, 1981.

Youd, Pauline. *Adopted for a Purpose.* Nashville: Abingdon Press, 1986 (Good reading with a spiritual application for children 8-12).

*Available from the National Committee for Adoption,
      Suite 326, 1346 Connecticut Avenue, N.W.
      Washington, D.C. 20036

Agency Listings

The following list of agencies should give you an idea of where to begin your adoption inquiries. Most of the agencies listed provide, along with other services, intercountry adoption placements, and many are religious organizations (noted with an asterisk). Service areas and requirements will differ with agency. It would also be wise to check with other couples who have adopted from the agency. Some agencies are more efficient than others, so find some satisfied adoptive parents before applying.

Dillon Southwest
P.O. Box 3535
Scottsdale, AZ 85257

*Globe Intl. Adoption, Inc.
6334 West Villa Theresa Dr.
Glendale, AZ 85308

Adoptions Intl. of Alabama, Inc.
1538 Wellington View Road
Birmingham, AL 35209

Bal Jagat—Children's World, Inc.
9311 Farralone Avenue
Chatsworth, CA 91311

Life Adoption Services
440 West Main Street
Tustin, CA 92680

Adoption Services Intl.
4737 Ortega Drive
Ventura, CA 93003

Bay Area Adoption Services
P.O. Box 2617
Sunnyvale, CA 94087

AASK America/Aid to Adoption of Special Kids
1540 Market
San Francisco, CA 94102

*Catholic Charities San Francisco
2045 Lawton Street
San Francisco, CA 94122

Family Connections
1528 Oakdale Road
Modesto, CA 95355

Adoption Horizons
P.O. Box 247
Arcata, CA 95521

Friends of Children of Various Nations, Inc.
600 Gilpin Street
Denver, CO 80218

Universal Family
315 South Clay
Denver CO 80219

*Hand in Hand International
4695 Barnes Road
Colorado Springs, CO 80917   Jewish placements, also.

Family Service, Inc.
92 Vine Street
New Britain, CT 06052

Heal the Children Northeast, Inc.
Box 129
New Milford, CT 06776

Intl. Alliance for Children
23 South Main Street
New Milford, CT 06776

The American Adoption Agency
1228 M Street N.W.
Washington, D.C. 20005

World Child
5121 Colorado Avenue N.W.
Washington, D.C. 20011

ASIA
7720 Alaska Avenue N.W.
Washington, D.C. 20012

The Barker Foundation
4114 River Road N.W.
Washington, D.C. 20016

Children's Services Intl.
1819 Peachtree Road #318
Atlanta, GA 30309

Homes for Children Intl.
1655 Peachtree Street NE, #1109
Atlanta, GA 30309

Illien Adoptions, Intl.
1254 Piedmont Avenue NE
Atlanta, GA 30309

Open Door Adoption Agency
P.O. Box 4
Thomasville, GA 31799

Adoption Center, Inc.
500 N. Maitland Avenue
Maitland, FL 32751

Universal Aid for Children
P.O. Box 610246
North Miami, FL 33162

Suncoast Intl. Adoptions
P.O. Box 332
Indian Rocks Beach, FL 34635

Adoptions in Idaho
P.O. Box 729
Post Falls, ID 83854

*Bensenville Home Society
331 South York Road
Bensenville, IL 60106

Travelers and Immigrants Aid of Chicago
327 LaSalle Street
Chicago, IL 60604

Adoption World
One E. Erie, #235
Chicago, IL 60611

Children's Home and Aid Society of Illinois
730 N. Main Street
Rockford, IL 61103

Hillcrest Family Services
1727 1st Avenue SE
Cedar Rapids, IA 52402

*Gentle Shepherd Child Placement Services
P.O. Box 1172
Olathe, KS 66061

Growing thru Adoption
P.O. Box 7082
Lewiston, ME 04240

*Intl. Christian Adoption Agency
60 W. River Road
Waterville, ME 04901

ACORN
10784A Hickory Ridge Road
Columbia, MD 21043

*Associated Catholic Charities of Baltimore, Inc.
320 Cathedral Street
Baltimore, MD 21201

Cambridge Adoption and Counseling Associates, Inc.
Box 190
Cambridge, MA 02142

Intl. Adoptions, Inc.
282 Moody Street
Waltham, MA 02154

World Adoption Services, Inc.
161 Auburn Street
Newton, MA 02166

Aliance for Children, Inc.
110 Cedar Street
Wellesley, MA 02181

Americans for International Aid and Adoption
877 S. Adams
Birmingham, MI 48011

Children's Hope Adoption Services
7823 South Whiteville Road
Shepherd, MI 48883

Foreign Adoption Consultants
P.O. Box 489
Kalamazoo, MI 49005

*Bethany Christian Services
901 Eastern Avenue NE
Grand Rapids, MI 49503

HOPE Intl. Family Services Inc.
421 Main Street
Stillwater, MN 55082

*Catholic Charities Archdiocese of St. Paul/Minneapolis
215 Old 6th Street
St. Paul, MN 55102

Children's Home Society of Minnesota
2230 Como Avenue
St. Paul, MN 55108

*Lutheran Social Services

2414 Park Avenue South
Minneapolis, MN 55404

Crossroads, Inc.
4940 Viking Drive, #388
Edina, MN 55435

Building Families Through Adoption
Box 550
Dawson, MN 56232

*Love Basket, Inc.
8965 Old Lemay Ferry Road
Hillsboro, MO 63050

Adoption Resource Center
R&R Health Services
2207 Park Avenue
St. Louis, MO 63104

Family Adoption and Counseling Services, Inc.
9378 Olive St. Road, #320
St. Louis, MO 63132

Worldwide Love for Children
1221 E. Republic Road
Springfield, MO 65807

Montana Intercountry Adoption, Inc.
109 S. 8th Avenue
Bozeman, MT 59715

Adoptions in Montana
554 W. Broadway, #557A
Missoula, MT 59802

Children of the World
855 Bloomfield Avenue
Glen Ridge, NJ 07028

Children's Services Intl., Inc.
P.O. Box 688
Long Valley, NJ 07853

Rainbow House Intl.
19676 Hwy 85
Belen, NM 87002

Family Resources
226 N. Highland Avenue
Ossining, NY 10562

Family Service of Westchester, Inc.
470 Mamaroneck Avenue
White Plains, NY 10605

Family Focus Adoption Agency
P.O. Box 388
Glen Oaks, NY 11004

Parsons Child and Family Center
845 Central Avenue
Albany, NY 12206

Adoption and Counseling Service, Inc.
1 Fayette Park
Syracuse, NY 13202

*Evangelical Adoption and Family Service, Inc.
201 S. Main St.
North Syracuse, NY 13212

*Covenant Children
P.O. Box 2344
Bismark, ND 58502

New Horizons Foreign Adoption Services, Inc.
2876 Woodland Place
Bismark, ND 58501

*Lutheran Social Services of Central Ohio
57 E. Main Street
Columbus, OH 43215

Spaulding for Children—Beech Brook
3737 Lander Road
Cleveland, OH 44124

Project Adopt
1613 N. Broadway
Oklahoma City, OK 73103

Small Miracles Intl., Inc.
7430 SE 15th, #220
Midwest City, OK 73110

*Dillon's Children's Services, Inc.
7615 E. 63rd Place So. #215
Tulsa, OK 74133

Plan Loving Adoptions Now, Inc.
P.O. Box 667
McMinnville, OR 97128

*Holt Intl. Children's Services
P.O. Box 2880
Eugene, OR 97402

*Tressler Lutheran Service Associates
25 W. Springettsbury Avenue
York, PA 17403

Welcome House
P.O. Box 836
Doylestown, PA 18901

Love the Children
221 W. Broad Street
Quakertown, PA 18951

The Adoption Agency
63 W. Lancaster Avenue
Ardmore, PA 19003

Adoptions Intl. Inc.
Benson Manor, #101
Jenkintown, PA 19046

Children and Home Study Associates
31 E. Franklin Street
Media, PA 19063

*Catholic Social Services
222 N. 17th Street, Room 329
Philadelphia, PA 19103

*Catholic Charities of Tennessee, Inc.
30 White Bridge Road
Nashville, TN 37205

*Holston United Methodist Home for Children
P.O. Box 188
Greenville, TN 37744

Adoption Resource Consultants of North Texas
P.O. Box 1224
Richardson, TX 75083

*Agape Social Services, Inc.
3200 Maple, #400
Dallas, TX 75201

Child Placement of Texas
615 N. 2nd Street
Killeen, TX 76541

The Care Connection, Inc.
400 Harvey Street
San Marcos, TX 78666

Rootwings Ministries, Inc.
P.O. Box 614
Barre, VT 05641

Pan American Adoption Agency, Inc.
12604 Kahns Road
Manassas, VA 22111

*Catholic Family Services
4206 Chamberlayne Avenue
Richmond, VA 23227

Family Services of Tidewater, Inc.
222 19th Street
West Norfolk, VA 23517

*Open Arms
16429 NE 133rd Court
Redmond, WA 98052

*Catholic Community Services
P.O. Box 22608
1715 E. Cherry
Seattle, WA 98122

Western Association of Concerned Adoptive Parents (WACAP)
P.O. Box 88948
Seattle, WA 98138

Adoption Advocates Intl.
658 Black Diamond Road
Port Angeles, WA 98362

Adoption Option, Inc.
1804 Chapman Drive
Waukesha, WI 53186

*Lutheran Social Services of Wisconsin and Upper Michigan
3200 W. Highland Blvd.
Milwaukee, WI 53208

Pauquette Children's Service
P.O. Box 162
315 W. Connant
Portage, WI 53901

The following agencies do not provide intercountry adoption placements, but they are established agencies you may wish to consider.

*Evangelical Child and Family Agency
1530 N. Main Street
Wheaton, IL 60187

*Sunny Ridge Family Center
2S426 Orchard Road
Wheaton, IL 60187

Golden Cradle Adoption Agency
2201 Route 38
Cherry Hill, NJ 08002

*Love Life Adoption Agency
P.O. Box 247
Florence, SC 29503

*Family Life Services, Inc.
520 Eldon Street
Lynchburg, VA 24501

*New Hope of Washington
1100 Lake City Way NE
Seattle, WA 98125

*Evangelical Child and Family Agency
2401 N. Mayfair Road
Milwaukee, WI 53226

Glossary

Adoptive mother and father: the woman and man who adopt and act as mother and father for an adopted child.

Birth mother: the woman who gave birth to the child.

Birth father: the man who fathered the child.

Gray market adoption: an adoption arranged through legal, but questionable, intermediaries. These adoptions may involve unusually large fees paid by the adoptive parents to the birth mother, attorney, doctor, and/or other intermediary.

Hard-to-place children: children other than healthy, white infants, including children over age six, minority or mixed race children, sibling groups, or physically or mentally handicapped children.

Home study: the written assessment of a couple's home, marriage, and personalities used by the social worker to evaluate potential adoptive parents.

Infertility: the inability to conceive a child after one year of unprotected intercourse.

Legal risk placement: children who are placed in adoptive homes at "legal risk" are not legally available for adoption at the time of placement because their birth parents have not yet relinquished rights, or the court has not yet declared them abandoned. Such placements run the risk of not being finalized.

Open adoption: an adoption arranged with the stipulation that the adoptive parents and birth mother meet at least once.

Secondary infertility: after at least one pregnancy, the inability to conceive after one year of unprotected intercourse.

Sibling Group: two or more children who are biologically related to one another.

Sub-family: the family unit formed within a sibling group after being transferred from one home to another. One child will usually begin to act as the "head" of the unit.